Truth Before Logic

Truth Before Logic

*Finding Wisdom with G. K. Chesterton
in a World Blinkered by Scientism*

MICHAEL B. MITCHELL

RESOURCE *Publications* · Eugene, Oregon

TRUTH BEFORE LOGIC
Finding Wisdom with G. K. Chesterton in a World Blinkered by Scientism

Copyright © 2024 Michael B. Mitchell. All rights reserved. Except for brief quotations in critical publications or reviews, no part of this book may be reproduced in any manner without prior written permission from the publisher. Write: Permissions, Wipf and Stock Publishers, 199 W. 8th Ave., Suite 3, Eugene, OR 97401.

Resource Publications
An Imprint of Wipf and Stock Publishers
199 W. 8th Ave., Suite 3
Eugene, OR 97401

www.wipfandstock.com

PAPERBACK ISBN: 979-8-3852-2092-2
HARDCOVER ISBN: 979-8-3852-2093-9
EBOOK ISBN: 979-8-3852-2094-6

VERSION NUMBER 09/09/24

To Gavin, Jordan, Aspen, Willa, and Rhett (John 6:27)

Contents

Preface | ix

Acknowledgements | xi

A Biographical Note | xiii

Introduction | xv

Chapter 1   The Contradiction of Scientism | 1

Chapter 2   Scientism, The Antithesis of Reason and Life | 14

Chapter 3   Truth Before Logic, The Test of Sanity | 30

Chapter 4   Beauty, Knowledge, and a Human Science that Excludes Humanity | 50

Chapter 5   The Human Mind Made for Myth | 65

Chapter 6   The Squib and the Stained Glass | 78

Chapter 7   Gratitude and the Grammar of God | 94

Chapter 8   That Which is Stronger Than Sorrow or Joy | 108

Bibliography | 127

Preface

ONE BRIEF CLARIFICATION WILL be important before beginning this book. The critique of the world blinkered by scientism offered in the following pages is not an attempt to depreciate the importance of scientific endeavors or dissuade anyone from trusting science to do what it is meant to do. As noted in the first chapter, scientific discoveries and technological developments over the past two hundred years have changed the world in glorious ways (for the most part), and we should all be deeply grateful for the ways these changes have enriched our lives. That which this book seeks to expose is the pop culture, folktale version of naturalist philosophy often called "scientism," which is a very different thing from science.

I was once invited by a friend to observe an Alcoholics Anonymous meeting. The night I attended happened to be the session focused on the importance of acknowledging a Higher Power in the recovery process. As the group members began to share their thoughts, one lady stood up and said that this was a particularly difficult part of the program for her because, as a child, she used to believe in God, but then she went to college and studied science and afterward could no longer believe. That is scientism!

As a guest, I would have been out of line to speak up, but I wanted to ask, what particular scientific discovery convinced her there is no God? What about the well-known PhD scientists at some of the world's most elite universities who are devout

Preface

Christians? What about the body of scientific discoveries which corroborate traditional concepts of a personal God?

The same woman had mentioned to the group how she had recently felt guilty for yelling at her kids. I also wanted to ask what insights science without God could give on what it means to feel guilty.

I didn't ask these questions, but if I had there likely would have been no response, because scientism isn't a well thought out set of beliefs based on clear evidence or clear convictions. It is a general sense about things—a cloud of sentiment about what well-educated people are supposed to believe. It is an attitude that is usually not put into words, but if someone were to try, it would be something to this effect: "People who lived a long time ago were ignorant, so they believed in gods and spirits, but we know about evolution and electricity. Since we know the world is billions of years old[1] and have air planes and iPhones, we know that God doesn't exist, and the only real things are the things that science can show us. All smart people believe this." This way of thinking can do to the souls of people and societies what a carbon monoxide leak can do to the occupants of a house, bringing about slow, imperceptible changes that undermine the ability to think and to live.

---

1. I do not believe an earth that is billions of years old is at odds with the teachings about God and creation in the Bible. What is at odds with scripture, reason, logic, conscience, consciousness, and our everyday experiences is the idea that the world is the product of an accident.

Acknowledgements

I would like to thank Richard Cleary, Bethany Wester, and Korey Llewelyn for their thoughtful critiques of the manuscript. I would also like to thank Dr. Jerry Walls, not only for his endorsement of this book, but more so for being one of the most inspiring teachers in all my years of higher education. I must also thank my wife, Leslie, for her constant love and support—for being a real-life Sarah Smith of Golders Green.

A Biographical Note

Gilbert Keith Chesterton was born in London in 1874 and died in Beaconsfield in 1936. He was a journalist, novelist, and philosopher, and one of the most influential writers of the twentieth century. His influence has continued through the decades after his death, and his insights are as relevant now as ever.

Much can be said about Chesterton's life, his jovial, child-like personality, and his vast body of work. For a detailed account of his talent and influence, I refer the reader to the "Discover Chesterton" page on the website for The Society of G.K. Chesterton. For those interested in an in-depth and comprehensive account of his life and works, see *G.K. Chesterton: A Biography*, by Ian Ker.

Here I will only say that the word genius is often loosely used to compliment a writer or thinker one is especially fond of, but true intellectual genius is a distinct category designating an elite mind. The intellectual genius is the cognitive equivalent of a professional athlete in that he or she operates at a level of ability which extremely few can match. The literary genius, in particular, is also able to communicate with a felicity that clarifies the opaque and simplifies the complex in a way that does not constrict but rather expands a reader's understanding. In this sense Chesterton was a true genius.

It's also true that one can be a genius and a callous, immoral, arrogant, person. One very significant factor in Chesterton's enduring influence is that he was a good man who genuinely invested his talents in pursuing what is good, beautiful, and true, and helped many others to do the same. A line from his essay in memory of the philosopher William James is indicative of his character and the character of his work: "One cannot teach a truth clearly if one is actually thinking about the teaching and not about the truth." Chesterton, who never earned an advanced university degree, is a shining example of the impact a person can make when his talent and success are used in service of the truth rather than the other way round.

Of the various ways he helped to fortify the minds of many against dangerous intellectual fashions, his perspective on the relationship between scientific and religious thought are especially important in the context of the early twenty-first century West. The proliferation of new technological capabilities and scientific discoveries creates the illusion that science alone can illuminate all aspects of human life, which is a belief that inevitably leads to a diminishing life. In such a context, Chesterton's insights can safeguard heart and mind from the danger of the soul-atrophy that results when the glaring success of science blinds us to the spiritual life for which science should be an instrument.

Introduction

IN THE INTRODUCTION TO HIS BOOK, *The Madness of Crowds*, Douglas Murray characterizes wealthy, modern Westerners as "the first people in recorded history to have absolutely no explanation for what we are doing here, and no story to give life purpose." Up until the modern era, human beings have moved through the natural world much like tourists in train cars. The train's point of departure and its destination were great mysteries, but the notion that it was on its way to somewhere definite was a given. Whatever terrain one may pass through, everything was understood in context of the journey.

Furthermore, the train was thought to make frequent stops in inhospitable places where passengers were required to face daunting challenges. And it was generally understood that one's conduct in the face of those challenges was a highly significant factor in determining what life would be like at the destination. Life was a story, and the story was a test and a journey. But, as Murray points out, modern Westerners no longer have a story and are consequently no longer on a journey. Focus in life oscillates between the bank and the bedroom, each with diminishing satisfaction in the absence of a metaphysical context to give meaning to the pleasures and pains of life.

For many in earlier eras, the idea that the human heart and mind *traversed* through the natural world—that the train moved on transcendent tracks imposed upon the natural elements like Union Pacific tracks laid in the desert—was a seemingly self-evident fact.

Introduction

But in the early twenty-first century, under the ostensible oracle of Science, we allegedly now know that there is no train. In light of the unprecedented knowledge of the double helix and the hippocampus, it is thought that "metaphysical"[1] is a contradiction in terms. Without pausing for the inconvenience of a cogent rationale, we celebrate the "heroic non sequitur"[2] that mastery of the physical world proves that there is nothing above or apart from the physical world.

It is now understood that we are not moving through or to anything of any significance beyond the physical properties that constitute our bodies and our environment. We are the first in the history of the world to have gotten off the train—the first to believe the train and the tracks are as random as the rocks that lie beside them.

This trajectory into the void was evident to C.S. Lewis a generation ago as he observed, "a single one-way progression"[3] of inquiry by which we begin to think of people as impersonal objects of scientific analysis. After learning that wind currents and not forest spirits sway the trees, we then apply the same logic to ourselves and begin to believe biochemical reactions and not human spirits move our bodies. This transition has had the ironic effect of simultaneously creating a mental atmosphere of intellectual superiority and an existential reality of spiritual poverty and psychological dysfunction.

Few deserve more credit for this triumphant contradiction than Nietzsche, who reveled in the liberation which he believed to be an inevitable result of the death of God:

> Indeed, at hearing the news that "the old god is dead," we philosophers and "free spirits" feel illuminated by a new dawn…finally the horizon seems clear again, even if not bright; finally our ships may set out again, set out to

---

1. One meaning of the prefix "meta" is over or above. If all of reality consists of the material properties and predictable physical forces which are accessible to the scientific method, then there can be nothing over or above the physical.
2. Jaki, *Chesterton, A Seer of Science*, 32
3. Lewis, "The Empty Universe"

Introduction

> face any danger; every daring of the lover of knowledge is allowed again; the sea, *our* sea, lies open again; maybe there has never been such an "open sea."[4]

As it turns out, such an open sea is a dismal, lonely sea of anomie. The sailor who is liberated from his captain, who has no destination and no coordinates, is free to create his own meaning. He can claim hundreds of nautical miles of saltwater as his own sovereign domain, but in doing so he is not free. He is pitiful.

And this is not just traditionalist rhetoric. A recent article in *Psychology Today* cites loneliness as "a new epidemic in the USA," referencing a study which found that loneliness can be as significant a factor in mortality rates as smoking and obesity.[5] This is poignant irony in light of the technological advancements over the past twenty years which have given people unprecedented means of staying "connected."

In 2018, the Prime Minister of the UK appointed a national Minister of Loneliness, explaining that "For far too many people, loneliness is the sad reality of modern life."[6] This is a telling reality coming from a nation which has transitioned culturally within the past hundred years from one of the most Christian to one of the most secular in the world. The fruits of Nietzsche's liberation are well articulated by one particularly observant Englishman, a medical doctor and cultural critic who observes that sixty years after the sexual liberation of the 1960's, relationships have become "kaleidoscopic in their changeability but oddly uniform in their denouement."[7] It is not hard to understand why loneliness has become an "epidemic" and a "sad reality of modern life" in a culture where Nietzsche is a sage and science is a religion.

People have been liberated from the confines of the metaphysical train and can now roam freely. But in the absence not only of a track but also of a destination we no longer see any reason to

---

4. Nietzsche, *The Gay Science*, 181-82.

5. https://www.psychologytoday.com/us/blog/envy/201902/loneliness-new-epidemic-in-the-usa, posted Feb. 12, 2019

6. Time Magazine, April 25, 2018

7. Dalrymple, "All Sex, All The Time," in *Our Culture, What's Left of It*.

Introduction

roam. We are fish who have freed ourselves from the fish tank, some having no idea how to find the ocean and others believing the ocean was a fable to begin with.[8]

In such a cultural and intellectual morass, few people will be more helpful in getting us back on the right track—back into the true story of humanity—than the boisterous, British journalist and philosopher G.K. Chesterton. In the pursuit of clear thinking and true flourishing, Chesterton appeals primarily not to logic but to sanity. In lucid contrast to the coronation of the scientific method as the chief arbiter of all important truths, he proposes the essence of human beings rather than the logical faculties we possess as the best starting point from which we can seek meaningful knowledge about ourselves and the world around us.

With great force of wit and wisdom, he shows that modern man has fastidiously observed all the phenomena in the world except himself. The fact that "man is not merely an evolution but rather a revolution"[9] is an insight from which he leads us into an approach to truth-seeking by which the most substantive and satisfying knowledge is to be found.

---

8. Chesterton, *The Poet and The Lunatics: Episodes in the Life of Gabriel Gale*, Kindle Location 627

9. Chesterton, *The Everlasting Man*, 26

CHAPTER 1

The Contradiction of Scientism

> "Now the trouble about trying to make yourself stupider
> than you really are is that you very often succeed."
>
> C.S. Lewis, *The Magician's Nephew*

FEW ENDEAVORS IN THE history of mankind have been more successful than the Scientific Revolution.[1] "Economic growth took off in the 1700s, starting in England, and has been accelerating ever since. [Economic historian Angus Maddison] estimates that the goods and services produced between 2001 and 2010 constitute 25 percent of all goods and services produced since A.D. 1."[2] There is no room for doubt; science works. Volumes upon volumes could be written on the stunning degree to which life has been impacted

---

1. The Scientific Revolution is generally defined as the era in the sixteenth and seventeenth centuries when the scientific method was codified and applied in new ways through the work of Francis Bacon, Rene Descartes, Isaac Newton, and many others. This is referred to as a "revolution" because of the unprecedented use and effectiveness of empirical observation and scientific reasoning which eventually led to the technological watershed of the Industrial Revolution.

2. "Quantifying History: Two Thousand Years in One Chart," Economist, June 28, 2011. http://www.economist.com/blogs/dailychart/2011/06/quantifying-history (Cited in the appendix, "Human Progress," in *Suicide of The West*, by Jonah Goldberg)

by the exponential surge in technological development in just the past 150 years. But success fosters illusion, and the greater the success the greater the illusion.

Scientific and technological developments have been overwhelmingly successful in meeting the practical needs of mankind, but such dazzling success has obscured the fact that mankind is not primarily a practical species. The practical should always be instrumental. The moment the practical becomes primary it becomes pathological, and a dominant pathology which has steadily crept into the minds of Western people over the past two centuries goes by the name of scientism.

Scientism is the idea that scientific inquiry is the only legitimate means of knowing what is true and real. It is the notion that if something can't be understood through empirical observation, scientific analysis, or mathematical calculation, it is either unknowable or not worth knowing. It is rooted in the philosophy of naturalism which holds that all of reality is reducible to matter and energy so that the idea of an immaterial reality is an oxymoron.

It is an assumption that pervades Western society, both explicitly and implicitly, through the teachings of a number of highly reputable and highly tendentious scientists.[3] Just as the success of a talented athlete can create the illusion in the minds of others (and in the athlete) that the same person would make a strong political leader, the success of talented scientific authorities in developing technology creates the illusion that they are also philosophical and moral authorities. Such is the propagating engine of scientism.

The general outlook of scientism is well articulated by Steven Pinker, one of its giddiest proponents: "The moral worldview of any scientifically literate person—one who is not blinkered by fundamentalism—requires a clean break from religious conceptions of meaning and value . . . The worldview that guides the moral and

---

3. It should be noted that Scientism has no monopoly on highly reputable scientists. Some of the most renowned scientists in the world are also religious believers: Francis Collins, John Polkinghorne, and Alister McGrath to name just a few.

The Contradiction of Scientism

spiritual values of a knowledgeable person today is the worldview given to us by science."[4]

This is what T.H. Huxley (aka "Darwin's Bulldog") described over a hundred years ago when he said, "The scientific method is the only method by which truth could be ascertained," and that "it is inevitable that [what is called] the scientific method must extend itself to all forms of enquiry."[5] This was the view of G.K. Chesterton's ideological adversary, Ernst Haeckel, who insisted that, "The remarkable progress in the natural sciences must perforce have had profound influence on the philosophy of thinking men," and that serious minded people must recognize a rigid distinction "between the clear dicta of reason in pure science and the nebulous imaginings of religion."[6]

Ironically, scientism itself is a religion, and the zeal of its priests and missionaries has not waned since Chesterton's time. It is a fundamentalist religion which poses a threat to the soul of Western civilization analogous to the threat Islamic suicide bombers pose to the infrastructures of Western civilization.

The sad influence of scientism has moved many into a state of mind much like that of an isolated Amazon tribesman who is taken to a large city for the first time where he observes someone preparing a meal in a well-equipped, modern kitchen. He's accustomed to spending hours preparing a meal with primitive tools over an open fire and so is understandably astonished at what he sees. But soon he becomes so enamored with refrigerators, microwaves, high-speed mixers, and air fryers that he loses any concern for eating.

In much the same way, many today are becoming more technologically astute and more psychologically and spiritually emaciated. We are infatuated with the tools and toys that enrich

---

4. Steven Pinker, *Enlightenment Now, The Case for Reason, Science, Humanism, and Progress*, (Viking Press, pg. 394)

5. Huxley, "Professor Huxley on Men of Science," *The Mechanics' Magazine*, 14 October 1871, 284-85.

6. Haeckel, *The Answer of Ernst Haeckel to the Falsehoods of the Jesuits Catholic* and, pg. 5

life with little concern for life. As the late Peter Berger explains, the secularization of the Western mind diminishes the horizons of thought and experience so that, "the reality of a middle-aged businessman drowsily digesting his lunch is elevated to the status of final philosophical authority." Such a shift of perspective, says Berger, results in "the triumph of triviality."[7] This being the case, the illusion created by posing the scientific method as the panacea for human ignorance and the golden key to fulfillment is an illusion from which we need to be sobered.

SCIENTISM AND GULLIVER'S TRAVELS

In the minds of many modern Westerners, science plays a role much like Jack Black's Gulliver in the 2010 film version of Gulliver's Travels. He arrives in Lilliput as a giant from a mysterious unknown land, a foreigner to the Lilliputians who are suspicious of him until he rescues the princess and saves the king. He is then hailed as "our savior," but then uses his new-found status to portray himself as something much greater than he really is, the noble and victorious President, The Awesome, from the island of Manhattan. The subjects of Lilliput, so enamored with his heroic acts, accept the audacious claims without questioning. Once the perception of Gulliver as an all-reliable authority is firmly established in the minds of the natives, they build an elaborate home for him and their imaginations are shaped by the (completely fabricated) lore of his personal history.

Likewise, the scientific method and a priority on disinterested logic arrived on the shores of Europe aboard the philosophical ships of Descartes, Bacon, and Kant, along with many others in the seventeenth and eighteenth centuries, introducing a way of thinking that was foreign to the natives. Up until that point, it had been generally understood that in speaking poetically about the most important things in life, "we may be speaking more accurately

---

7. Berger, *A Rumor of Angels*, 84

The Contradiction of Scientism

than when we speak analytically."[8] The vast majority of mankind had understood that all the good things in life most accurately described as *real* are rooted in a place that is "not a realm which can ever be discovered with charts and telescopes and syllogisms."[9]

But the scientific method, deploying disinterested[10] logic in the pursuit of knowledge and mastery over the material world has made every day human experience practically efficient, physically comfortable, and financially prosperous in ways and to a degree that would have been unimaginable to anyone living prior to the early modern era. Because of these heroic feats that moved the world from covered wagons to space exploration in a disproportionately short time, we tend to think of science and technology not simply as life-saving tools but as an all-encompassing, life-directing authority which holds a privileged place not only in pragmatic questions, but also in politics, ethics, and theology.

If this seems overstated, one need only consider the number of times "science," "scientists," and "scientific studies" are cited in advertisements for commercial goods, or how many times politicians and activists seek to persuade others with a call to "follow the science." In the conceptual framework of the post-Enlightenment West, science has shifted from a pragmatic method of inquiry to a nebulous authority, so that the word "science" makes a similar impression on the minds of many modern people as the phrase "The Crown" once made on the minds of medieval English subjects. The authority of the monarchy was comprehensive over all aspects of life. The monarch was understood to be a sovereign in the strict

---

8. Howard, *Chance or the Dance? 2nd Edition: A Critique of Modern Secularism*, p. 6

9. Howard, *Chance or the Dance? 2nd Edition: A Critique of Modern Secularism*, p. 20

10. "Disinterested logic" is a helpful enough phrase in referring to the common conception of scientific reasoning. However, it should be kept clear in mind that nothing that is purposefully deployed can be truly disinterested; there must first be an interest in the thing for which logic is deployed in order for it to be deployed to begin with. If a scientist is truly "disinterested" toward a subject he would never have enough interest to engage in scientific inquiry to begin with. For more on this see Chapter 1 of Michael Polanyi's *Personal Knowledge*.

sense and questioning the legitimacy of The Crown was to set oneself at odds with an immutable authority—to step outside the boundaries of the world in which wise and decent people live.

The concept of science as an omnipotent sovereign is made explicit in the quotes from Steven Pinker and T.H. Huxley cited above: "The worldview that guides the moral and spiritual values of a knowledgeable person today is the worldview given to us by science."[11]—"The scientific method is the only method by which truth could be ascertained. It is inevitable that [what is called] the scientific method must extend itself to all forms of enquiry."[12]

However, the fundamental flaw that is to the worldview of scientism what that infamous north Atlantic iceberg was to the Titanic is precisely the enthroning of science as a *worldview* that extends to "all forms of inquiry." This is the problem which Chesterton so artfully exposes as a fissure in the foundation of the science-only paradigm.

One of the sobering impacts of Chesterton's work is a clarification of the often wide gap between scientific and philosophical insight. The proponents of scientism are so consumed with examining the processes of scientific inquiry and application, and so enamored with its successes, they feel no need to consider more fundamental philosophical questions. Their myopic perspective makes them like a man who has long been frustrated over constantly losing his car keys and then proudly tells his friends that he's found a foolproof solution: he'll lock them in the car. He has solved the initial problem but also created another set of problems which are far worse, and he has done this because he focuses only on the pragmatic problem of locating the keys and not on the metaphysical question of the purpose of keys and cars and the importance of arriving at the places they are designed to take him.

In the flurry of increasingly sophisticated and practically effective technology, secular scientists either do not take time to

---

11. Steven Pinker, *Enlightenment Now, The Case for Reason, Science, Humanism, and Progress*, (Viking Press, pg. 394)

12. Huxley, "Professor Huxley on Men of Science," *The Mechanics' Magazine*, 14 October 1871, 284-85.

The Contradiction of Scientism

consider or give absurd answers to important philosophical questions: What is the nature of the mind which is so passionately motivated to seek knowledge for its own sake? What is the fundamental essence of the individual will which judges the endeavor of science to be more worthy of one's attention than other pursuits? What is the origin and essence of the standard by which one makes moral judgments about the use and misuse of technology? It takes little reflection to see that these deeply important questions lie well beyond the scope of scientific inquiry.

Those who, like Steven Pinker, live and think only within "the worldview given to us by science" are characterized by the same myopic bravado as those in Chesterton's time who sought to reform the laws about (and thus the essence and practice of) marriage:

> The chief thing to say about such reformers of marriage is that they cannot make head or tail of it. They do not know what it is, or what it is meant to be, or what its supporters suppose it to be; they never look at it, even when they are inside it. They do the work that's nearest; which is poking holes in the bottom of a boat under the impression that they are digging in a garden. This question of what a thing is, and whether it is a garden or a boat, appears to them abstract and academic. They have no notion of how large is the idea they attack; or how relatively small appear the holes that they pick in it.[13]

The fundamental problem with the early twentieth-century marriage reformers was a void of metacognition. Their scope of consciousness did not extend beyond their immediate task. In much the same way, rapid progress in scientific digging evokes an excitement and self-satisfaction that inoculates the intellectual curiosity necessary to consider the context in which the digging is done, and thus the purpose of digging to begin with. The science-only view is blind to the fact that no deliberate human endeavor ever takes place outside of a metaphysical[14] framework. The whole endeavor

---

13. Chesterton, *The Superstition of Divorce*, Ch. 1
14. The term "metaphysical" can be used in at least two ways. Here I intend

of science is clear evidence of this, a point ironically acknowledged by T.H. Huxley who "once admitted that seeing continuous gradations among all species, classes, orders, and phyla is a metaphysical vision."[15]

Apart from basic biological functions induced by survival instinct, all human actions take place within, and are guided by, a conceptual framework in which an Ultimate Good holds a place at the top of a hierarchy of value. It is the hierarchical framework—particularly the priority at the top around which all else is oriented—that determines the significance and purpose, the methods and practice, the definitions of success and failure, in science and in every other human enterprise. Science is a human pursuit, but scientism is an amnesiac mindset which does not account for the deepest factors of the spiritual, human values which motivate the pursuit of scientific knowledge. Without these science as a field of study would not exist. To use Chesterton's phrase, those who seek to explain every aspect of human experience through science "do the work that's nearest" without slowing down to consider what it is about the nature of the work that resonates with the nature of the scientist.

The devotees of scientism propose a world of uninterpreted facts which are perceived by various human minds; the religion-tainted mind, either corrupt or naïve, "interprets" the facts according to subjective biases, while the scientific mind simply perceives the facts as they are. Therefore, the scientific minds are the more noble because they are the ones best aligned with the truth. The problem, however, is that the idea that prioritizing truth over bias is a noble trait is itself an interpretation. One immutable aspect of the human mind which makes a mechanistic, naturalist worldview incoherent is value attribution. From the moment we wake up every morning we select from an infinite range of options and choose to focus on certain things which are worthy of our attention. We either know inherently or we simply decide that some

---

it the most literal sense as that which is over (meta) the physical.

15. Huxley, "Biogenesis and Abiogenesis" (1870), in *Discourses: Biological and Geological*, 256-57

things—scientific study, for example—are more valuable than others. This awareness or choice about what is most valuable comes first. We only "put our mind to" doing something after the mind has decided that the thing is worth doing.

GENERAL EDWARD EDWARDIAN AND AN OVERCONFIDENT PARANORMAL INVESTIGATOR

There are few better examples of those with a science-only worldview "doing the work that's nearest" with no awareness of a more fundamental reality than the argument proposed in a 2017 TED talk, "A Scientific Approach to the Paranormal," given by Carrie Poppy, a radio host and paranormal investigator. In the talk, which has now garnered approximately 2.4 million views, she explains some disturbing phenomena experienced upon entering her home—hearing spooky wind noises, feeling a distinct sense of dread as if she was being watched, and a physical pressure on her chest. She naively suspects these as signs of a haunting and even resorts to a spiritual cleansing ritual burning sage to repel evil spirits.

She then consults a group of skeptics who suggest that her home is not haunted by a ghost but poisoned by a carbon monoxide leak. She calls the gas company to investigate and is told by the technician, "It's a really good thing that you called us tonight, because you could have been dead very soon," a point which evokes a response of sympathetic triumph from the audience. This liberating disillusionment is the epiphany that leads to her job as an investigative reporter focused on scientific explanations of alleged paranormal activity. She goes on to explain the conclusion drawn from her work which is the culminating insight of the talk: "I've done over 70 investigations like this. I would love to tell you that nine times out of ten, science wins, saves the day, it's all explained. That's not true. [Rhetorical pause] The truth is, ten times out of ten, science wins, it saves the day!" As one might expect, this triggers a swell of applause from the scientifically minded congregation at the TED talk, though it's unlikely that any who were so impressed with the exposure of the fiction of supernatural realities realized that their reaction itself is clear evidence of a supernatural reality.

The contradiction comes into sober light when we consider the question, what exactly does science "win" and what are we saved from when science "saves the day"? It is clear that we are allegedly saved from superstition and confusion, and the victory won is that of truth over falsehood. Such victory is thought to come when one learns that all events believed to be caused by supernatural entities[16] actually have purely mechanical causes which are completely accessible to the scientific method. In short, the claim is that spiritual beings (which almost certainly don't exist) cannot affect physical things. The problem is that she makes this argument by explaining how she exerted her spiritual will to affect her physical brain in pursuing her investigative work. In choosing to acknowledge the greater value of one thing (the truth) over another (personal bias), Ms. Poppy supernaturally affects material objects with spiritual force—the force of her will. As C. S. Lewis explains,

> If we are in fact spirits, not Nature's offspring, then there must be some point (probably the brain) at which created spirit even now can produce effects on matter not by manipulation or technique but simply by the wish to do so. If that is what you mean by magic then magic is a reality manifested every time you move your hand or think a thought.[17]

She is commended by the audience for her intellectual honesty, which is the honorable trait of aligning her beliefs with the facts even when the facts are contrary to her preconceived notions. While fools would rather believe a happy lie than a disturbing truth, she, on the other hand, values the truth and the audience applauds her virtue. She is praiseworthy while those who choose familiarity and comfort over truth are derelict.

---

16. "Supernatural entities" meaning efficacious, intentional powers whose existence cannot be reduced to material properties.

17. Lewis, *Miracles*, 198

The Contradiction of Scientism

But the elephant in this room of naturalist philosophy is the fact that, without an undetermined, spiritual will—that is, a capacity for decision making distinct from inevitable natural causes—there can be no such thing as moral praise for intellectual honesty or blame for intellectual cowardice, because there can be no such thing as choice.

This may at first seem like question begging: "You only say she exerted her spiritual will in making a choice because you start with the assumption that a human being is a spirit, not just a body." But this misses the more fundamental and logically necessary point. The concept of will is, by definition, spiritual. If will can be fully explained by determined, mechanical phenomena, then it is not will. This is why a number of materialist philosophers argue that there is no such thing as free will.[18]

To make a choice is to attribute value to one thing over another. For many, the security and emotional gratification gained from comforting but false beliefs is more valuable than the truth. Such people would rather believe a happy lie than a disturbing truth. In Ms. Poppy's case, she ostensibly values the truth over her previously held beliefs, and it is for this judgment that she is commended as a virtuous person. But making *good* judgments and acting accordingly requires wisdom and a will to act which cannot be reduced to neuro-mechanical brain activity. The very concept of good judgment as a virtue is unintelligible apart from an immaterial, undetermined, personal will which could have judged differently, or could have abdicated the responsibility to judge altogether and acted only to gratify animal appetites.

This may sound like a philosophically controversial point, but it is a matter of fact confirmed in common experience. If a man gets thoroughly drunk at a party, for example, and says to someone he's barely met, "I love you." or "Have you always been that fat?" another person—a friend, perhaps worried for the man's safety—would likely say, "Don't take him seriously. He doesn't mean it. It's the alcohol talking." This is a common enough scenario to be

---

18. Sam Harris, Jerry Coyne, William Provine, and Sean Carrol, are a few among several others who deny the reality of free will.

cliché, and it illustrates the inviolably spiritual nature of a person. The mere idea that we shouldn't take a drunk person's words seriously clarifies, like lightning in a black sky, the distinction between the chemical and the person. We know that the words of an intoxicated person are suspect because the words are attributed to a chemical (alcohol) rather than to a person. It's not *him* talking. The thoughts the words express are not originating from *his* mind, or at least not from his "right mind."

Words are only meaningful if they come from the heart, that is to say from the spiritual will or intent of the individual. It does not matter whether it's the alcohol talking or the natural-chemicals-in-the-brain-since-birth talking. If one believes that human beings are entirely reducible to and determined by chemical relationships, then every word any person ever says is just as nonsensical and meaningless as the words of a drunk person. As the naturalist philosopher, Sam Harris, says about the ability to choose one's outlook and behavior, "There is no extra part of me [apart from spiritless matter] that could decide to see the world differently."[19]

If this is the case, then the appropriate response to every word ever spoken is, "Pay no attention. That's just the chemicals talking." But, of course, we're then left with the very tricky problem of taking seriously the words of the person telling us that all other words are only caused by mindless chemicals. When someone admonishes us to drop our belief in a spiritual will and attribute everything about human beings to bio-chemicals, there is always an implicit expectation that we make an exception for the one speaking. Every time someone makes an argument, every time we speak the truth to counter falsehoods, every time we declare with conviction, "*I* mean it! With all my heart!", we are making emphatic and pronounced our spiritual nature which can no more be attributed to atoms and chemicals than a man sacrificing himself in battle can be attributed to a nervous reflex. Medals are not given to commemorate an excess of adrenaline. White gowns and wedding rings are not poetic expressions of reproductive hormones.

19. Harris, "The Illusion of Free Will," https://www.samharris.org/blog/the-illusion-of-free-will

The Contradiction of Scientism

Those who take pride in their sober mindedness for forcing spirit and matter into a zero-sum game bring to mind another character from Jack Black's Gulliver's Travels. General Edward Edwardian is jealous of Gulliver, but his attempt to establish his superiority backfires when he tries to use language from Gulliver's world that he doesn't understand:

Gulliver (unaware that Edward is approaching from behind): "This Edward guy seems like kind of a lame ass."

Edward, indignantly: "A lame what? It is my impression that 'lame ass' is a negative expression from whence you came. If this is the case, you shall be thrown into stocks!"

Gulliver: "No, no, no, no. 'Lame ass' means great, brave, courageous, heart-of-a-lion man."

Edward: "Then I am not just a lame ass. I am a big lame ass."

Gulliver: "The biggest!"

Edward: "I, General Edward Edwardian, am the biggest lame ass in all of the land!"

People who think they are exposing the impossibility of spiritual will affecting physical matter by triumphantly proclaiming, "Ten times out of ten science wins!" are playing General Edwardian's role in reverse. He has a delusion of grandeur, comically exposed by his ignorance of a certain phrase; naturalist philosophers have a delusion of degradation, ironically exposed by the zeal of their arguments. Their claim that humans are bodies and not spirits is undermined by the obvious spiritual passion of their argument.

CHAPTER 2

Scientism, The Antithesis of Reason and Life

> "Statements are made so plainly and positively that men have hardly the moral courage to pause upon them and find that they are without support."
>
> G.K. Chesterton, *The Everlasting Man*

CONTINUING IN THE SAME vein as their ideological forefather who touted the death of God as the liberating event which sets us free to sail on an open sea, naturalist philosophers like Steven Pinker appeal to reason as the supreme antidote which can sober us from the confusion of religious superstitions, and the sole means of personal and social euphoria:

> [Through reason we can] enjoy the gift of mutual benevolence with friends, family, and colleagues . . . you have the responsibility to provide to others what you expect for yourself. You can foster the welfare of other sentient beings by enhancing life, health, knowledge, freedom, abundance, safety, beauty, and peace. History shows that when we sympathize with others and apply our ingenuity to improving the human condition, we can

Scientism, The Antithesis of Reason and Life

make progress in doing so, and you can help to continue that progress.[1]

This is a point where the importance of philosophical assessment and its embarrassing absence in the works of certain Ivy League professors becomes evident. Though Steven Pinker uses the word "reason" in this passage, the more appropriate word is science (though, of course, science depends on reason). According to his own argument, he cannot mean reason because the essence of reason is supernatural.[2] In appealing to the authority of reason, a true philosophical naturalist exemplifies the kind of inherent contradiction in the sentence, "I would like to have a nuanced discussion with you, but I'm afraid that won't be possible because I don't speak a word of English."

Our faculty of reason is just that, a faculty. It *facilitates* the illumination of reason just as the members of a school *faculty* facilitate the illumination of learning. The faculty members themselves are not the object, as if Professor Smith is synonymous with the noun, "knowledge," or Faculty Member Jones with "learning." Likewise, learning takes place within certain buildings which we call "facilities," but the building in which learning takes place and the learning are two different things.

The root word comes from the Latin words, *facilis* and *facer*, which mean "easy" and "make do." The role of academic faculty is to make knowledge more easily accessible. A faculty is a means of access to a certain power, but the power itself is something distinct from that which enables access to it. Our brains constitute much of our faculty of reason. Thus, our brains enable us to comprehend or "see" what is reasonable—that is, our brains facilitate reason by enabling us to see it. In a similar way that the power of electricity illuminates a light bulb, the power of reason illuminates our brains. Just as the light bulb is not, itself, electricity, my brain is not, itself, reason. Like love and ideas, the essence of reason is immaterial.

---

1. Pinker, *Enlightenment Now, The Case for Reason, Science, Humanism, and Progress*, 3-4

2. "Supernatural" here only meaning that reason is something that cannot consist of material properties.

Naturalist philosophers often appeal to a behaviorist or functionalist theory of mind by which they define reason as the physiological state and processes of the brain. In that case, reason simply is how the brain functions; reason is nothing more than what the brain is and does. But this too is incoherent in light of the fact that what *ought* to be cannot be derived from what *is*. Yet, Pinker and like-minded naturalists are some of the loudest voices admonishing us of our moral obligation to think and behave rationally in contrast to those who are "blinkered by fundamentalism." We are told incessantly that reason is an authority we *ought* to obey. They are apparently unaware of the principle in C.S. Lewis's maxim, "Unless the measuring rod is independent of the things measured, we can do no measuring."[3]

With appropriate irony, the Latin root for *faculty* and *facilitate* is also the root for *facile*. The dictionary definition of facile is, "appearing neat and comprehensive only by ignoring the true complexities of an issue; superficial." This is an apt description of scientism and naturalist philosophy more generally. In divorcing themselves from "religion" and touting the marriage of science and naturalism as the sole means of "knowledge, freedom, abundance, safety, beauty, and peace," they are like a man living on the coast of Florida who finally gets fed up with the oppressive heat and constant threat of hurricanes and so decides to move to The Bahamas.

Like it or not, the inherent value in things like reason, justice, freedom, beauty, and peace is a transcendent (non-physical) value and no less so because we are able to experience these in increasing measure through science and technology and other physical faculties.

KNOWLEDGE BEYOND PROOF

The enthroning of scientific reasoning as the only means of true certainty inevitably creates a doctrinaire attitude of superiority toward claims of knowledge in the absence of empirical or logical

---

3. Lewis, "The Poison of Subjectivism"

proof. When confronted with those who believe that there is a personal God, that all people will have a conscious existence after the death of their bodies, or that the law of morality is as immutable as the law of gravity, the devotee of scientism may feel like an urbane business executive listening to his country cousin drone on about UFOs or a nefarious collusion between big pharma and the new world order.

However, this reflexive dismissal of claims that can't be empirically proven is itself the result of irrational conditioning. The rigid rationalist may be prone to think of those with certain-but-unprovable religious beliefs as being only a few degrees separated from flat-earthers or bigfoot conspiracy theorists, but the psychological process which leads people to perceive claims of supernatural realities this way is much like the process by which Christian fundamentalists are conditioned to automatically think of beer or dancing as inherently evil.

If "evidence" in William Clifford's maxim that, "It is wrong always, everywhere, and for anyone, to believe anything upon insufficient evidence,"[4] is taken to mean tangible, demonstrable evidence, then any claim to certainty that cannot be empirically or logically demonstrated will be instantly perceived as benighted and facile, just as one who believes that alcohol is of the Devil will instantly perceive someone with a pint of Guinness at a checkout counter as a lost soul flirting with eternal perdition. In each case, a passionate commitment to false assumptions distorts perception.

Before going further, a clarification about the nature of proof and its relation to knowledge will be helpful. One common thinking error which results from overexposure to scientism is the conflation of proving and knowing. Often implied by the retort, "You can't prove that!" is the claim, "You can't really know that!" Clifford's poignant epigram so quicky resonates with our rigidly logical, post-Enlightenment minds that we easily miss the fact that evidence and proof are not the same thing.[5] Proof

---

4. Clifford, "The Ethics of Belief"

5. For one of the most thorough and erudite explanations of how belief in God is warranted apart from a rigid, Cartesian chain of inference or

requires evidence that is publicly demonstrable, but not all evidence is. If I were to see a bear while hiking alone on an alpine trail, I would know that the bear exists and that it roams on that particular mountain. I would also know the inner emotional and physiological experience caused by personally encountering a bear in the wild. My knowledge of these facts would be as certain as the knowledge that I am typing on a keyboard as I write this paragraph. All of this would be completely certain and completely unprovable. Too many modern thinkers glibly dismiss claims of certainty about the existence of God, for example, only because it cannot be proven in a strict sense, but the fact that a certain kind of knowledge is unprovable (as almost all knowledge is) does not diminish it as true knowledge: "Some hold the undemonstrable dogma of the existence of God; some the equally undemonstrable dogma of the existence of the man next door."[6] Knowing is not contingent on proving.

A crucial but easily missed point is that axioms are necessary but cannot be logically demonstrated. No conversation, argument, or communication of any kind could ever take place if every premise had to be proved beforehand. I believe, for example, that there is a Moral Law which is objectively real and distinct from the human mind. It's not hard to imagine debating this with a skeptical opponent who believes all moral codes are the product of cultural or biological conditioning and are therefore relative and never absolute. We may be willing to debate the matter, but we can only debate if my faculty of reasoning works on the same rational principles and acknowledges the same rules of logic as hers. But how can she know this is the case?

It is not logically contradictory to think that my faculty of reason evolved through a chaotic concoction of accidental-and-inert-but-nonetheless-increasingly-sophisticated matter in such a way as to use words of a common language but with opposite meanings and with an opposite thought process from that of other speakers. What if, in my rational framework, the word, "Hello" is

---

mathematical proofs, see Alvin Plantiga's *Warranted Christian Belief*.

6. Chesterton, *Heretics*, 130

a brazen insult, and "I'd like to discuss this with you" means something like "skunks are tastier than antelopes."?

If my philosophical opponent wants assurance that our debate will be a meaningful exchange, she must first get logically sound verification that what I mean by the words in my vocabulary—not just the technical jargon but even the most basic phrases—are generally the same as what she means by the same words. But seeking that kind of confirmation would be just as unwise (and just as difficult) as refusing to get out of bed until it can be proven that standing upright won't dislodge an undetected blood clot which will be fatal before reaching the bathroom.

Also, how does my philosophical sparring partner know that the whole debate isn't just a ruse, that I'm not actually a covert agent working for a sinister organization who seeks to rid the world of people who ask philosophical questions? I would appear to be a curious, philosophically minded person just like her, but that's exactly how such a covert agent *would* appear. Along with the logical confirmation that our faculties of reason and language coincide, she also must find a way to rule out the possibility that I am working undercover with nefarious motives.

Back to the point I would defend in the hypothetical debate, inevitably, those who would oppose the claim of a Moral Law do so because they believe claims of moral absolutes are used as a means of oppression. But then the idea that it is immoral to use false claims to oppress people is, of course, a moral absolute. Trusting in the absence of logical proof that my interlocutor is not a covert agent, or a shape-shifter, or an actor paid to exploit me, is absolutely necessary for me to have a meaningful conversation with her. I cannot prove that these things are not true, but I am nonetheless completely rational in believing that she is who she appears to be.[7] The closest thing to an inviolable logical confirmation of axioms is the realization that one would live in a state of insanity if she didn't take them for granted.

---

7. For a more thorough treatment of the explanation between the relationship between proof and belief, see Alvin Plantiga's *Warranted Christian Belief*.

KNOWLEDGE THAT PRECEDES PROOF

Proof, in a scientific sense, has to do with the reliability of a process. If the process is faulty or incomplete then, it is thought, we can't legitimately claim to know the thing in question. But this notion is based on false assumptions which can affect our minds much as a severe vitamin deficiency would affect our bodies. It is the pervasive assumption that knowledge inaccessible to the process of scientific demonstration is not real knowledge. As Chesterton's contemporary, Joseph McCabe, explained, "The worldview that guides the moral and spiritual values of a knowledgeable person today is the worldview given to us by science."[8]—"Physical science has revolutionized our view of our environment, and is rapidly filling up the lacunae in a mechanical conception of the universe on which men would base their inferences of a spiritual world."[9]

The quote from McCabe is particularly revealing. The problem with the proposition that men only base inferences of a spiritual world on lacunae in the "mechanical conception of the universe" is that it fails to realize that the deepest, most significant spiritual knowledge is not inferred. A similar contradiction stands out in the quote from Steven Pinker cited earlier. If "science" means a mode of acquiring knowledge though observation and inference, then, by definition, we could never get moral and spiritual values from science. This is a category mistake, like trying to find the molecular structure of loyalty. Moral and spiritual values are not items that present to our empirical senses for observation in order for us to calculate and predict their utility. The knowledge inherent in moral convictions does not come about through a process of observation and inference, and it is not *acquired* like a knowledge of car engines.

A morally sensitive conscience and clear scientific analysis have one thing in common. As mentioned in the first chapter, the same pre-calculative knowledge which is necessary to see

---

8. Pinker, *Enlightenment Now, The Case for Reason, Science, Humanism, and Progress*, 394

9. Joseph McCabe, *From Rome to Rationalism or Why I Left The Church*, 4

self-evident moral realities is also necessary for the practice of good critical thinking and thus good science. A thinking person is a knowledge-seeking creature who pursues proofs, evidence, and logical validation, and a conscientious person is one who seeks to scrutinize his perceptions to discern the ways bias might skew his moral judgments. But the knowledge that having true beliefs and right convictions is important is already present in the mind of the person prior to the act of observation and the process of discernment. The morally sensitive mind comes before moral theories. The truth-prioritizing mind comes before the logical validation of an argument.

The fundamental convictions that distinguish a sane person from a sociopath make for particularly compelling evidence of this kind of inherent, prerequisite knowledge. If someone with a healthy conscience were walking down a dark city street and suddenly peered into a secluded alley to see a boy with Downs Syndrome being beaten by a man twice his size, that person would instantly know that he was witnessing an evil act. But this kind of knowledge does not come as the result of a process of reasoning. One simply *sees* that it is evil. Such an awareness is a basic characteristic of a healthy conscience. It is a self-evident fact that powerful people abusing weaker people is immoral. However, self-evident does not mean that something is so obvious that it is impossible to miss. It means that something is so obvious that one has to be pre-conditioned by irrational bias or undisciplined carnal passion not to see it. Self-evident facts can be screened out by certain influences which incentivize us to be blind.

It is often argued that even though a knowledge of good and evil is inherent in conscience, our consciences are the product of our social-cultural atmosphere, so that the sensitivities of conscience are a product of conditioning. But if this were the case then we could have just as easily been conditioned in opposite ways. If it's true that our sense of moral obligation and our basic understanding of the difference between good and evil is not grounded in an objective, transcendent reality, but instead comes about only through the psychological weather of our social environment, then some could have developed a conscience which sees the man in the alley as virtuous because of his strength and assertiveness and the mentally disabled boy as deserving of his punishment because of his weakness.

One of the problems with this is that it does not comport with the nature of the experience of conscience. To experience conscience is to know that it "implies a relation between the soul and something exterior, and moreover, superior to itself; a relation to an excellence which it does not possess, and to a tribunal over which it has no power." [10] The nature of conscience is that of an authority we cannot control. If I mentioned to a friend that I'd been struggling with a guilty conscience because of an insensitive remark made to a coworker, it would be nonsense for the friend to reply, "Well then, just change your conscience and you'll feel better." This cannot be done, because conscience is an authority which is necessarily external to oneself.

THE INCONGRUITY OF SCIENTISM AND HUMAN FLOURISHING

Considering a distinction in two ancient Greek words for life makes further sense of the problem with scientism. *Bios* is the root word for the English *biography* and *biology*. It is the data of life, the sequence of events and the mechanical processes of our bodies and the world around us. *Zoe* is the spiritual life. It describes our convictions, commitments, loyalties, longings, loves, and hatreds. Bios describes the weight and diameter of the heart; *zoe* describes the singing or breaking of the heart.

According to naturalistic philosophy *zoe* is an illusion and is only ever a manifestation of bios. As explained by physicist, Sean Carroll, a self-described naturalist, "there is only one realm of reality, the material world, which obeys natural laws, and ... we human beings are part of it."[11] In stark contrast, a vast number of human

---

10. Boekraad and Tristram, *Arguments from Conscience*, 113 (Cited in *The Soul's Upward Yearning*, by Robert Spitzer, pg. 74)

11. https://www.preposterousuniverse.com/blog/2012/05/07/the-case

beings who lived before the dawn of the scientific age believed in another world. They understood that when their hearts jumped at the sight of a lion or a lightning bolt, and when their hearts sang at a first kiss or broke at the death of child, that this was because the natural phenomena they could feel and see were imbued with a power and significance from a realm they could not see.[12]

In using logic at the expense of wisdom, scientism proposes that if only ancient people had the advantages of a scientific education, they would have known that the deep sense in the human mind that life is *about* something is an illusion. They would have understood that all notions of a purpose greater than the survival of the species are only illusions generated by the same kinds of processes that produce vomit and vertigo. According to the science-only worldview, the human body is a machine full of tiny micro-machines, and the body is itself one micro-component of a much larger machine which we call Nature. There is nothing before, after, or apart from the machine. "There is only one realm." To suggest otherwise is unscientific. Machines do what machines do. That is all. In other words, believers in scientism sacrifice zoe on the altar of bios, and in so doing obscure the kind of life that makes human life humane.

Contemporary scientism evokes a reaction similar to that of The President of Nicaragua in Chesterton's *The Napoleon of Notting Hill*, as he responds to the description of an efficient and unceremonious government void of ritual and tradition:

> "I don't know that I have any particular objection in detail to your excellent scheme of Government. My only objection is a quite personal one. It is, that if I were asked whether I would belong to it, I should ask first of all, if I was not permitted, as an alternative, to be a toad in a

---

-for-naturalism/

12. More accurately to many ancient ways of thinking, there was no rigid distinction between natural and supernatural. Most everything was thought to be what modern people call "supernatural."

ditch. That is all. You cannot argue with the choice of the soul."[13]

The revulsion which makes one prefer to live as a toad in a ditch than in a purely mechanical world does not register with devotees of scientism because very few of them think their philosophy all the way through. They appear to be oblivious to the necessary implications of what they claim to believe. Many scientists like Sean Carrol who believe "there is only one realm of reality, the material world," appear to flourish in their work with a keen sense of purpose, and yet, buoyant and evasive as bees in a hailstorm,[14] they somehow fail to see that the idea of a completely material universe nullifies the concept of purpose and thus makes human flourishing impossible.

One of the most common responses to this criticism stems from the existentialist philosophy proposed by John Paul Sartre—that each individual must create his own purpose. The problem with this is that the kind of purpose that satisfies the deep longing for a purposeful life entails the pursuit of living up to expectations placed on us by an authority higher than ourselves. Experiencing the fulfillment of a meaningful life comes in the knowledge that we did (or are doing) what we're *supposed* to do. But according to Sartre and other atheists who find great purpose in their lives, what we're supposed to do is nothing more than whatever our instincts move us to do. This is a flat contradiction, which is why the idea that one can find meaning in creating his own purpose is just as reasonable and fulfilling as choosing to create his own college degree or military rank.

In light of the advice Chesterton gives for arguing with a madman—that when "dealing with a mind that was growing morbid, we should be chiefly concerned not so much to give it arguments as to give it air, to convince it that there was something cleaner and cooler outside the suffocation of a single argument."[15]—the most

13. Chesterton, *The Napoleon of Notting Hill*, 18
14. This phrase is taken from a character in *The Curate's Awakening*, by George Macdonald.
15. Chesterton, *Orthodoxy*, 24

formidable counter to reductionistic scientism is to bring it out of the sterile, monochrome hue of the lab into the vibrant light of the multifaceted, living reality of conscious human experience. In this light it becomes clear just how incommensurate the science-only worldview is with the deepest desires of the human soul.

CHESTERTON THE SABOTEUR

This same truncated science which strains the gnat of superstition while swallowing the camel of nihilistic self-contradiction was evident in some of Chesterton's contemporaries as well, and it is in his response that we begin to see a much larger horizon of knowledge. Along with the proposition of a completely mechanical universe, his opponent, Joseph McCabe, believed, like many others, that a commitment to reason requires one to reject "first the mysterious rites and dogmas of Christianity, then its sacred literature, and, finally, even the positions of natural theology."[16]

McCabe's point here brings the unsettling naivete of scientism out of the forest into the clearing. He and his twenty-first century ideological progeny seem to say, "Ha! Belief in a spiritual world can only be maintained in the ignorance of scientific discoveries. It is only from the lacunae in the mechanical conception of the universe that religious people infer a spiritual reality. But such lacunae are rapidly shrinking in the light of scientific discovery, and soon those ignorant religious believers will see the nature of the universe is completely mechanical and in no way spiritual. There are no spirits, only machines!"

What this fails to realize is that, just as a body without a spirit is a dead body, a world without spirit is a dead world. This is a fact so fundamental to everyday experience it feels silly to argue the point. Common assertions like, "He's got a head for the business but his heart's not in it," or "Every note was played with precision, but she was just going through the motions," are nonsensical if there is no qualitative distinction between spiritual and mechanical

16. Joseph McCabe, *A Sketch of The Progress of The Rationalist Spirit In The Nineteenth Century* (Watts & Co. (Watts & Co., 1897) pg. 6

reality. "Going through the motions," is one of the most common English phrases for describing dead, spiritless, mechanical activity. "Mechanical" is an epithet when applied to humans because we know that human life is a spirited life, and yet, a purely mechanical world is thought to be an uplifting and liberating discovery!

Chesterton explains that the problem with this view of life is that it screens out everything that's truly alive:

> Take first the more obvious case of materialism. As an explanation of the world, materialism has a sort of insane simplicity. It has just the quality of the madman's argument; we have at once the sense of it covering everything and the sense of it leaving everything out. Contemplate some able and sincere materialist, as, for instance, Mr. McCabe, and you will have exactly this unique sensation. He understands everything, and everything does not seem worth understanding. His cosmos may be complete in every rivet and cog-wheel, but still his cosmos is smaller than our world. Somehow his scheme, like the lucid scheme of the madman, seems unconscious of the alien energies and the large indifference of the earth; it is not thinking of the real things of the earth, of fighting peoples or proud mothers, or first love or fear upon the sea.[17]

It's not just that certain facts are screened out by the material-mechanical view, but that these are the very facts that define human life. This is the cost of scientism: It devises a world in which human beings can exert complete control only by obscuring the aspects of life which are essential to human flourishing. It takes no account (or gives absurd accounts) of human nature. It bypasses the things that matter most in life and consequently forgoes the possibility of true flourishing and fulfillment.

This explains much of why modern Westerners are "the first people in recorded history to have absolutely no explanation for what we are doing here, and no story to give life purpose."[18] The things which give life purpose are love, beauty, morality, and God,

---

17. Chesterton, *Orthodoxy*, 27
18. Murray, *The Madness of Crowds*

Scientism, The Antithesis of Reason and Life

none of which can be reduced to inert matter which can be calculated and controlled.[19] In trying to convince us that matter is "all there is, or ever was, or ever will be,"[20] the pseudo authority figures of scientism seek to shoe-horn spiritual creatures into a "purely mechanical universe" which is smaller than our world.

They seem to have neither the logical integrity nor the stomach to face the conclusions of their own argument. In contrast to the naïve notion of utopia Steven Pinker envisions as the inevitable result of reason without God, and Joseph McCabe's gleeful description of a dead, mechanical world, their fellow atheist, Bertrand Russell, didn't succumb to the temptation to whitewash the conclusion which is the necessary implication of naturalist philosophy:

> Such, in outline, but even more purposeless, more void of meaning, is the world which Science presents for our belief. Amid such a world, if anywhere, our ideals henceforward must find a home. That Man is the product of causes which had no prevision of the end they were achieving; that his origin, his growth, his hopes and fears, his loves and his beliefs, are but the outcome of accidental collocations of atoms; that no fire, no heroism, no intensity of thought and feeling, can preserve an individual life beyond the grave; that all the labors of the ages, all the devotion, all the inspiration, all the noonday brightness of human genius, are destined to extinction in the vast death of the solar system, and that the whole temple of Man's achievement must inevitably be buried beneath the debris of a universe in ruins—all these things, if not quite beyond dispute, are yet so nearly certain, that no philosophy which rejects them can hope to stand.[21]

---

19. Even this sentence would be incoherent within a purely material world. Inert matter cannot move or control itself. Neither can it make calculations about itself. Therefore, concepts like controlling and calculating are imposed on the world of inert matter from a different kind of existence.

20. Carl Sagan, from the 1980 video series *Cosmos*. Sagan makes this point about the cosmos.

21. Russell, "A Free Man's Worship," first published as "The Free Man's Worship,"

Russel's obvious but unusually honest conclusion reveals the emptiness of the cheery vision of a golden age of progress achieved by irreligious rationality. There is no way to put a positive spin on an existence that is inevitably hurtling toward nonexistence. Of all the necessary ingredients for peace and fulfillment, existence is definitely a non-negotiable.

The dizzying speed of technological development blinds the devotees of Scientism to the inevitable annihilation of "the whole temple of Man's achievement." They are much like a character from Chesterton's novel *The Flying Inn*, Mr. Hibbs, who has,

> a great talent for one of the worst tricks of modern journalism, the trick of dismissing the important part of a question as if it could wait and appearing to get to business on the unimportant part of it. Thus, he would say, "Whatever we may think of the rights and wrongs of the vivisection of pauper children, we shall all agree that it should only be done, in any event, by fully qualified practitioners."[22]

In much the same way, those like Steven Pinker who triumphantly tout humanist progress against the backwoods bent of "progressophobia"[23] while at the same time jettisoning God and immortality are essentially saying: "Yes, of course, there is the fact that we, all of our achievements, and all the love and joy we have ever known will cease to exist in the oblivion of the supernova, but we should take great satisfaction in the dramatic reduction of the child mortality rate in the past century and the invention of the iPhone."

In responding to such comi-tragic blindness, Chesterton works like a saboteur behind the scenes in the theater of scientism. The actors play the part of austere, intrepid arctic explorers in front of a cardboard backdrop painted to resemble an inhospitable landscape against which they courageously stake out the only rational dwelling place for the future of humanity. But then the saboteur

---

22. Chesterton, *The Flying Inn*, 51

23. See the chapter by this name in Pinker's *Enlightenment Now, The Case for reason, Science, Humanism, and Progress*

knocks the supports out from behind the set and golden sunlight streams over the audience as the backdrop falls to reveal happy picnickers in a rolling green field under a rich blue sky.

Such a change is brought about by realizing that any chain of logical reasoning that leads to a true conclusion about purpose and meaning in life must begin not with things observed by the five senses, but with the axioms of human consciousness and conscience. Russel's proposition that all conscious human life is destined to oblivion can be construed as the end of an inductive chain of reason, but it is a conclusion that is fundamentally at odds with the things we know prior to any inductive process.

It is at this point that one of Chesterton's most significant insights comes into view. For him the starting point of epistemology—the point from which we begin to get an accurate picture of reality—is not a concern for undeniable empirical observations or for what can be confirmed through an indubitable chain of inference, as important as these are. Rather, primary to a concern for observation and computation is the question of what a human being is. The following chapter will consider in greater detail the kind of knowing Chesterton says, "is not a logical thing but a primary and direct experience," which is more fundamental and comprehensive than our capacity for observation and calculation.[24]

---

24. Chesterton, *The Everlasting Man*, 73-74

CHAPTER 3

Truth Before Logic, The Test of Sanity

"The man who cannot believe his senses, and the man who cannot believe anything else are both insane, but their insanity is proved not by any error in their argument, but by the manifest mistake of their whole lives."

G.K. Chesterton, *Orthodoxy*

SARTRE SAID A PERSON has no essence when he is born, "because to begin with he is nothing. He will not be anything until later, and then he will be what he makes of himself."[1] Nietzsche believed this too, and it is a reasonable suspicion that such a belief was a contributing factor to the state of mental incoherence in which he spent the last decade of his life. It is a philosophy at odds with sanity. The foibles of Nietzsche and Sartre's existentialism make for a clarifying back drop against which Chesterton's contribution to philosophy stands in sharp relief. One of his great insights is that sanity, rather than logical consistency, is the primary benchmark by which theories and arguments should be assessed.

Sanity is a kind of axiomatic vision. It is a state of mind defined by the ability to see certain fundamental realities primary to any demonstration or explanation. The seeing (or believing) nature

1. Sartre, *Existentialism is a Humanism*

of the mind is the necessary precondition for the process of reasoning.² Like roads that must first be in place before one can drive a car, the conscious, seeing mind—that is, the distinctly human mind—is the orderly system of highway infrastructure on which the vehicle of logic is driven. Thinking that logical consistency is sufficient apart from certain first principles is like thinking a car is sufficient without a road. As is often said of people who are out of touch with reality, those who deny the pre-logical knowledge of human consciousness are "off track" or "in their own world." They get stuck in the mud or drive in circles while everyone else is cruising along on the freeway.

As the Chesterton scholar, Duncan Reyburn, explains, "Hermeneutics [interpretation] is always first a matter of being before it is a matter of knowing. It is a matter of some metaphysical or ontological grounding before it is a matter of epistemology."³ The essential insight obscured by enthroning the scientific method as the immutable emperor of verification is that human cognition occurs within a range of different perceptions and experiences of which logical computation is only one.

Because sanity and good judgment require one's use of logic to be framed by the more basic aspects of cognition, logical thinking severed from the full range of human consciousness—what Chesterton calls "reason used without root"⁴—is the intellectual equivalent to a SCUBA diver severed from his oxygen tank:

> Such is the madman of experience; he is commonly a reasoner, frequently a successful reasoner. Doubtless he could be vanquished in mere reason, and the case against him put logically. But it can be put much more precisely in more general and even aesthetic terms. He is in the clean and well-lit prison of one idea: he is sharpened to one painful point.⁵

---

2. Kaufman, 'Between Reason and Common Sense,' *Philosophical Investigations*, 28. 2005, 144

3. Reyburn, *Seeing Things as They Are: G. K. Chesterton and the Drama of Meaning*, 42.

4. Chesterton, *Orthodoxy*, 32

5. Chesterton, *Orthodoxy*, 32

Such a prison can be thought of as a prison of proof in which one is locked away from the primary knowledge of things which form a web of understanding apart from which logically demonstrable facts have no meaning.

THE NECESSITY OF UNSCIENTIFIC KNOWLEDGE

The assumption that we cannot have strong confidence in anything which cannot be observed, controlled, quantified, and predicted makes us human equivalents of a sophisticated bird who is too astute to believe in air because air cannot be presented to the senses of a bird in the way that a tree branch or a telephone pole can. Wise birds understand that even though air can't be seen as a tangible object, the fact that there is no option for an airless life for a bird makes air a necessary reality. We should believe not only that which is logically demonstrable, but more fundamentally, that which we would be insane not to believe whether or not the truth of such a belief can be demonstrated through a chain of inferential reasoning. There are certain realities that cannot be proven but must be believed in order for a person to live and think in a way which is consistent with the essence of what a human being is—in other words, in order to be sane.

Chesterton's point about the difficulty of arguing with a madman highlights the essential importance of a certain pre-logical knowledge which must guide our use of logic:

> If you argue with a madman, it is extremely probable that you will get the worst of it; for in many ways his mind moves all the quicker for not being delayed by the things that go with good judgment. He is not hampered by a sense of humor or by charity, or by the [mute] certainties of experience.[6]

A sense of humor, an obligation to charity, and the mute certainties of experience are essential factors in good judgment, and yet the necessity of these cannot be explained in a logically comprehensive

6. Chesterton, *Orthodoxy*, 23

way. They are irreducible facts about human consciousness. If someone dismisses or diminishes the importance of these because they cannot be demonstrated with a syllogism, he becomes more logical and less sane. Thus, "the madman is not the man who has lost his reason. The madman is the man who has lost everything except his reason."[7]

As Rayburn explains about the illogical inclination for play, "Play, understood as referring to an intense absorption in the constraints of the ordinary, initiates us into a more fundamental mode of being in the world than what is allowed for by the Cartesian prioritization of what is presumably fully disclosed to our conscious minds."[8]

It is precisely the "more fundamental mode of being" to which Chesterton turns our attention. This is a mode of being—primary to a process of logical inference—from which sane people see realities which are essential to human flourishing. As noted in the previous chapter, he suggests responding to the madman's argument not by proposing a counter argument but by drawing attention to a greater, more expansive reality, "not so much to give it arguments as to give it air, to convince it that there was something cleaner and cooler outside the suffocation of a single argument."[9] He goes on to explain what the madman and the rigid rationalist have in common:

> Just as I am affected by the maniac, so I am affected by most modern thinkers. That unmistakable mood or note that I hear from Hanwell,[10] I hear also from half the chairs of science and seats of learning to-day; and most of the mad doctors are mad doctors in more senses than one. They all have exactly that combination we have noted: the combination of an expansive and exhaustive reason with a contracted common sense. They are universal

---

7. ibid

8. Reyburn, *Seeing Things as They Are: G. K. Chesterton and the Drama of Meaning*, pg. 30

9. Chesterton, *Orthodoxy*, 24

10. An English insane asylum

only in the sense that they take one thin explanation and carry it very far.[11]

That common sense which is being contracted is the sense that comes from the primary mode of being in which we are aware of certain realities in an axiomatic way. On the one hand there is an existential knowledge which is primary to a logical process of inference—a knowledge and will which are the instigating agents and directors of the logical process—and on the other, conclusions which are drawn as the result of a chain of inferential reasoning.

This makes sense of why his response to the madman's argument is not to critique his logic but to show him a compelling reality which his narrow logic has screened out. We may not be able to present a logically irrefutable counterargument to the madman's claim that he is Christ or the King of England, but there is a knowledge deep in the human soul by which a person knows that such claims cannot be true regardless of how logically defensible they may be. This is not a matter of rejecting logic but of appreciating its limits.

SUBTERRANEAN KNOWLEDGE

Two of the most important points about a knowledge that precedes logic are that such knowledge is constantly assumed in our everyday behavior, and that we are psychologically dependent on it. In his book, *A Rumor of Angels*, Peter Berger illustrates this by approaching the question of God and life after death by considering common human behavior rather than philosophical arguments.

In a chapter titled "Theological Possibilities: Starting with Man," Berger makes a case for what he calls "inductive faith":

> I use induction to mean any process of thought that begins with experience. . .
> By "inductive faith," then, I mean a religious process of thought that begins with facts of human experience.[12]

---

11. Chesterton, *Orthodoxy*, pg. 27
12. Berger, *A Rumor of Angels*, 64

Upon examining these facts of human experience, he concludes that certain characteristics of basic human behavior display "signals of transcendence," which he defines as "phenomena that are to be found within the domain of our 'natural' reality but that appear to point beyond that reality."[13]

One such phenomena is hope and its relationship to happiness. As Berger explains, "Human existence is always oriented toward the future. Man exists by constantly extending his being into the future, both in his consciousness and in his activity."[14] Not only does our perspective constantly extend into the future, but in a way that is beyond the reach of anything that can be clearly, immediately demonstrated from empirical observation. We instinctually conceive of the future in hope.

To illustrate this, Berger proposes a scenario where the mother of a young child wakes in the middle of the night to the sound of the child's screams as he is having a nightmare in the next room. The mother rushes to the child's bedside, lifts him out of bed, cradles him to her shoulder, pats his back and says . . .

Though I stopped short of completing the sentence, likely the reader has already completed it in his or her mind. What the mother says to the child is, of course, "It's okay. It's okay. It's going to be alright." It's hard to imagine a more common and predictable scene. But Berger follows with a provocative and telling question. Is the mother lying to the child? This may sound insensitive, but it is a very important question. What the mother definitely does not mean in telling the child "It's going to be alright" is that the nightmare wasn't real and that the child has several decades of life to live before he ceases to exist. This is actually the opposite of what she means, but if there is no reality beyond what we can know through empirical, scientific observation, then it is, indeed, a fact that all human roads lead to the unconscious abyss that will inevitably result when the sun runs out of energy. Berger argues that unless "The religious interpretation of the universe" is correct, then the mother is lying to the child because conscious existence

---

13. Berger, *A Rumor of Angels*, 59
14. Berger, *A Rumor of Angels*, 68-69

ending forever at some point in the future does not comport with any reasonable definition of "alright."

Chesterton makes a similar point in opposing what he calls "carpe diem religion." In contrast to a perspective that encourages one to make the most of that which is fleeting, he argues that real happiness in an experience is only possible when it is believed that the experience will in some way endure:

> The carpe diem religion is not the religion of happy people, but of very unhappy people. Great joy does not gather rosebuds while it may; its eyes are fixed on the immortal rose which Dante saw. Great joy has in it the sense of immortality; the very splendor of youth is the sense that it has all space to stretch its legs in.[15]

The idea that the temporal, fleeting nature of something increases the propensity for enjoyment is a contradiction. "If we are to be truly [happy], we must believe that there is some eternal [happiness] in the nature of things."[16] One of the most compelling points that makes the scenario of the mother and child a "signal of transcendence" is the fact that no matter how much one depends on scientific observations to inform our beliefs about ultimate reality, we *must* believe that, despite the perpetual decay that surrounds us, somehow things will be alright.[17] Hope for the future is as necessary for a healthy mind as water is for a healthy body. A lack of hope is a fundamental symptom of mental pathology, and one of the most common factors in chronic depression and suicidal ideation.

If a person truly believes, as Bertrand Russel so clearly explains in the infamous quote cited earlier, "that all the labors of the

---

15. Chesterton, *Heretics*, 43

16. Chesterton, *Heretics*, 44

17. Regarding the basic claims of Christianity, such as the historical factuality of the events in the life of Christ and the fidelity of the text of modern Bibles to ancient manuscripts, there is a vast body of scientific research which is highly supportive of the basic claims of Christian theology, but Berger's point in the cited chapter is to set aside evidence of this kind and focus only on the implications of everyday human behavior.

ages, all the devotion, all the inspiration, all the noonday brightness of human genius, are destined to extinction in the vast death of the solar system," then he would be forced to conclude, along with Russell, that the plight of human beings is one of "unyielding despair."[18]

However, it seems that such a person would be moved to reconsider his philosophy in view of the incongruity of a purely material world which science tells us will inevitably end in death, and yet is nonetheless filled with people who have the strongest possible disgust at the thought of death, and whose happiness depends on the hope of eternal life. Peter Berger puts the point forcefully in referring to a consensus among psychologists that "though we may fear our own death, we cannot really imagine it . . . a 'no' to death is profoundly rooted in the being of man."[19]

That "no" is rooted in our being because we are aware of an eternal reality that is inaccessible to the scientific method. This is why Bertrand Russell who claimed that our beliefs should only be formed by science, and that the world science reveals is ultimately one of "unyielding despair," still continued to vigorously pursue knowledge as a philosopher and justice as a passionate anti-war activist. Regarding the latter, one wonders how the obliteration of all the inspiration and genius of humanity by a nuclear war in the present could be any better or worse than obliteration in the future implosion of the solar system? Like so many others, Russell's intellect claimed fidelity to science alone, but he appears to have lived by another set of principles. As Pascal said, "the heart has reasons the reason knows not of."[20]

A generation before Russell, Dostoyevsky illuminated this tension between the knowledge of the heart and the rigidly logical intellect in his atheist character, Ivan Karamazov.

In one of the most significant dialogues in the book, Ivan tells his saintly brother, Alyosha,

---

18. Russell, "A Free Man's Worship," first published as "The Free Man's Worship," Dec. 1903
19. Berger, *A Rumor of Angels*, 70
20. Pascal, *Pensee*

> Do you know I've been sitting here thinking to myself: that if I didn't believe in life, if I lost faith in the woman I love, lost faith in the order of things, were convinced in fact that everything is a disorderly, damnable, and perhaps devil-ridden chaos, if I were struck by every horror of man's disillusionment—still I should want to live and, having once tasted of the cup, I would not turn away from it till I had drained it! At thirty, though, I shall be sure to leave the cup, even if I've not emptied it, and turn away—where I don't know . . .
>
> The centripetal force on our planet is still fearfully strong, Alyosha. I have a longing for life, and I go on living in spite of logic. Though I may not believe in the order of the universe, yet I love the sticky little leaves as they open in spring. I love the blue sky, I love some people, whom one loves you know sometimes without knowing why.[21]

Ivan says he goes on living, continuing his thirst for life, "in spite of logic," but the logically inaccessible truth known in the heart is not against but rather above logic, as the experience of wonder at the sight of a star is above a knowledge of the gasses that comprise it.

THE CUBE OF SANITY AND THE SQUARE OF LOGIC

If sanity is represented by a cube, then logic is an essential square on one side. Sanity refers to a healthy mental state of which logic is only a part, just as bodily health is the greater reality of which digestion is only a part. A person can have a perfectly functioning digestive system and yet be unhealthy, and a person can have a keen capacity for logic and yet remain blind to the most important truths. In a brief article in the London Daily News, Chesterton explains how the use of good logic does not necessarily lead to a knowledge of truth:

---

21. Fyodor Dostoyevsky, *The Brothers Karamazov*, Book Five, Chapter Three

Truth Before Logic, The Test of Sanity

> The relations of logic to truth depend, then, not upon its perfection as logic, but upon certain pre-logical faculties and certain pre-logical discoveries, upon the possession of those faculties, upon the power of making those discoveries. If a man starts with certain assumptions, he may be a good logician and a good citizen, a wise man, a successful figure. If he starts with certain other assumptions, he may be an equally good logician and a bankrupt, a criminal, a raving lunatic. Logic, then, is not necessarily an instrument for finding truth; on the contrary, truth is necessarily an instrument for using logic —using it, that is, for the discovery of further truth and for the profit of humanity. Briefly, you can only find truth with logic if you have already found truth without it.[22]

Just as the process of logical deduction must maintain internal consistency in order to be valid, logic must also maintain a consistency with the realities known through human consciousness and experience which are beyond the reach of logic. Chesterton refers to an awareness of such realities as "common sense" because it is a kind of knowledge common to most people regardless of their IQ.

As he explains in "Defense of Penny Dreadfuls," those who, from a sense of intellectual superiority or an overdependence on scientific verification, reject the moral tropes of lowbrow literature—which are the "maxims of daily life—can be high in culture and low in sanity:

> The vast mass of humanity, with their vast mass of idle books and idle words, have never doubted and never will doubt that courage is splendid, that fidelity is noble, that distressed ladies should be rescued, and vanquished enemies spared. There are a large number of cultivated persons who doubt these maxims of daily life, just as there are a large number of persons who believe they are the Prince of Wales; and I am told that both classes of people are entertaining conversationalists.[23]

---

22. Chesterton, "Straight Thinking," London Daily News, February 2, 1905
23. Chesterton, *The Defendant*, "A Defense of Penny Dreadfuls."

Likewise one does not need intellectual sophistication to see the good sense in shaking hands, though a rigid logician may scoff at the absurdity of greeting someone by grabbing part of his body and erratically moving it up and down. Common sense sees clearly that it is right to wrap presents and dance at weddings, though the cold logician rolls his eyes at the wastefulness (The paper doesn't change the contents of the package, after all, and couples are just as married if they don't dance). Common sense knows the value of the rapport developed through small talk despite its superficial content and the value of another person's presence when the weight of heart and mind are too heavy for words to bear.[24] Such is the knowledge of sanity, a knowledge that is to calculating logic what Shakespeare is to Morse Code.

Why do acquaintances comment on inconsequential and obvious facts about the weather? What sense is there in visiting a grieving person when you have no words to say and no way to bring their loved one back? Logic sealed off from all the other aspects of human understanding makes these kinds of behaviors appear absurd. But to those who see in light of all the various facets of human awareness, the one who believes only what logic can confirm is absurd. We might say such a person "isn't all there," because he is missing all the other capacities of perception that make us well rounded adults who are generally able to see things as they are.

The well rounded mind—that is, the mind informed by facts from around the spectrum of experience and awareness—is a precondition for good judgment, which is why Chesterton says,

> We do not in the least wish that our particular law-suit should pour its energy into our barrister's games with his children, or rides on his bicycle, or meditations on the morning star. But we do, as a matter of fact, desire that his games with his children, and his rides on his bicycle,

---

24. For more on this argument, see Thomas Howard's explanation of the difference between the "old myth" and the "new myth" in the first chapter of his *Chance or The Dance*.

and his meditations on the morning star should pour something of their energy into our law-suit.[25]

If a man stopped for speeding explains to the officer that he has just been notified of his child's sudden illness and that he was speeding to get to the hospital, if the officer's response is "Sorry, sir, but the law is the law," he would be rightly derided as "robotic" or "inhumane," because he would be making a judgment in light of only one facet of a multifaceted situation, obscuring the most important (and most human) aspects of the situation by focusing solely on the legal or logical.

As with Chesterton's barrister, we would hope that the police officer's games with his children and his meditations on the morning star would inform his judgment in deciding how best to apply the law to the distressed man. This is how well-informed decisions are made "from the full human point of view."[26] It is true that making decisions based only on emotions unchecked by logic typically leads to regret, but it is also true that making decisions based only on logic untempered by emotion and conviction leads to regret. It also leads to an ironic intellectual malaise in which people understand less while priding themselves on how clearly they understand.

EXAMPLES OF LOGICAL INSANITY

There are times when an argument can be made most effectively by simply allowing one's opponents to articulate his beliefs. Few things could more forcibly demonstrate Chesterton's point that good logic can be involved in crime and lunacy than the beliefs of those who enthrone science and logic at the expense of a fully human point of view. Those who genuflect to science as an Omnipotent Sovereign develop a mindset which is something like scientific autism. Just as many autistic people are brilliant in their ability to remember minutia about the history of sports cars or

---

25. Chesterton, *Heretics*, 104
26. Chesterton, *Heretics*, 99

dinosaurs but are at a complete loss when it comes to simple, personal interactions, those blinkered by scientism obsess over a scientific mode of analysis to the point that they become blind to some of the most obvious and important realities on which basic human dignity and sanity depend.

Few examples demonstrate this with more disturbing clarity than an argument made by the ardent atheist, Sam Harris, in his work on free will. Because Harris is committed a priori to the assumption that anything inaccessible to the scientific method cannot be real, he rejects belief in free will because there is no room for it in a world comprised only of predetermined, interlocking mechanical causes.

To make his point he recounts a heinous crime in Connecticut in 2007 in which two men broke into a family's home, bound the father to a chair, stole $15,000, performed lewd acts on an 11-year-old girl after tying her to her bed, raped and murdered the mother, and then set the house on fire while the 11-year-old and her 17-year-old sister were still tied to their beds.

Even though the capacity for moral decision making doesn't show on an MRI, every sane person knows that what these two men did was evil. They were not forced to commit the crime; they could have chosen differently and are, therefore, accountable. But Sam Harris is too scientifically enlightened to believe that people make moral choices. (A curious thing given his shrill indignation toward religious types whom he so often deems immoral). I could not write a more damning critique of Harris' hyper-logical scientism than his own words in explaining his thoughts on "the illusion of free will" as it relates to the crime:

> Whatever their conscious motives, these men cannot know why they are as they are. Nor can we account for why we are not like them. As sickening as I find their behavior, I have to admit that if I were to trade places with one of these men, atom for atom, I would *be* him: There is no extra part of me that could decide to see the

world differently or to resist the impulse to victimize other people.[27]

Harris' argument that people aren't actually people but soulless automata programmed by their DNA brings to mind a remark from Chesterton on G.B. Shaw's ideological commitment to the notion of progress:

> Having come to doubt whether humanity can be combined with progress, most people, easily pleased, would have elected to abandon progress and remain with humanity. Mr. Shaw, not being easily pleased, decides to throw over humanity with all its limitations and go in for progress for its own sake.[28]

Likewise, when confronted with a moral reality that doesn't comport with Sam Harris' preconceived scientific paradigm, with a narrow-mindedness which dwarfs that of the most rabid Christian fundamentalist, he rejects the reality and keeps the paradigm. Harris is the madman who has lost everything except his reason!

Along with Harris' denial of moral accountability in heinous crimes, the infamous Princeton professor, Peter Singer, makes for a stark example of logical insanity. In his *Practical Ethics*, Singer infamously gives a chillingly cool-headed defense of infanticide:

> At present parents can choose to keep or destroy their disabled offspring only if the disability happens to be detected during pregnancy. There is no logical basis for restricting parents' choice to these particular disabilities. If disabled newborn infants were not regarded as having a right to life until, say, a week or a month after birth it would allow parents, in consultation with their doctors, to choose on the basis of far greater knowledge of the infant's condition than is possible before birth.[29]

There may be no "logical basis" for restricting parents from killing their week-old baby. Nonetheless, blindness to the heinousness of

---

27. Harris, "The Illusion of Free Will"
28. Chesterton, *Heretics*, 104
29. Singer, *Practical Ethics*, 2nd Ed., 190

such an act is a sure sign of insanity. It is the absence of this kind of pre-logical, moral knowledge that defines a sociopath. The fact that sociopaths can be highly intelligent without a moral conscience is a crucial point because it highlights the fact that conscience and logic are two distinct categories.

Conscience is a faculty of perception analogous to eyesight. In the light of conscience, one "sees" the basic difference between good and evil. Through conscience we know with utter certainty that children are precious, life is sacred, death is an abomination, and justice *must* be done. The person with a good conscience and bad logic may pursue the defense of children and the execution of justice in ineffective or inefficient ways; the person with a bad conscience and good logic may work to kill children and build an empire of injustice with the highly efficient, mechanical precision of Auschwitz.

In another passage from *Practical Ethics*, Singer reveals with unflinching candor the moral vertigo that results from elevating logic at the expense of other ways of knowing.

> A week-old baby is not a rational and self-conscious being, and there are many nonhuman animals whose rationality, self-consciousness, awareness, capacity to feel, and so on, exceed that of a human baby a week, a month, or even a year old. If the fetus does not have the same claim to life as a person, it appears that the newborn baby does not either, and the life of a newborn baby is of less value than the life of a pig, a dog, or a chimpanzee.[30]

How does one know the difference between a newborn baby and a pig or a dog? By what faculty of perception does a person see a different inherent value in a human baby than in a non-human animal? The lens of logic alone doesn't always make that difference clear, therefore Singer sees no clear difference.

He shows how logic can be used as a vehicle whose direction is determined by its driver. In keeping with the sense of his argument, we could show, with quite a formidable body of evidence, that certain Ivy League intellectuals are not as rational and

---

30. Singer, *Practical Ethics*, 122-23

self-conscious as some children and thus argue that children be allowed to give input on the granting of tenure to Princeton professors. With just as much logical consistency, it could also be proposed that adults with PhDs are more rational and self-conscious than adults with Downs Syndrome, so those with PhDs should be allowed to form committees to decide whether the intellectually disabled are worthy of the valuable resources spent for their benefit or if it would be best to eliminate them. The vehicle of logic can take a person in many directions when there is no authoritative metaphysical map to guide the way.

FACTS OBSCURING TRUTH

Peter Singer, Sam Harris, Steven Pinker, Richard Dawkins, T.H. Huxley and so many others who have naively imbibed the notion that "The scientific method is the only method by which truth could be ascertained,"[31] illustrate with stunning clarity the kind of inhumane myopia that can result from a logic-only approach to truth. They are like a man who concludes that whales are no more real than unicorns because neither can be seen with a microscope and then rolls his eyes at anyone ignorant enough to question his methods.

Chesterton counters this by proposing a holistic approach to seeking truth which involves all aspects of a person discerning all aspects of the reality one seeks to know. He challenges a data-obsessed scientism with the proposition that facts can obscure truth, so that knowing the truth about something requires a consideration not only of isolated facts but also of the greater reality of an atmosphere which gives facts a context of meaning.

A concern for the composite reality of the general character of a person or situation makes Chesterton's approach distinct from that of the rational method of crisp inferences from one fact to another characteristic of Sherlock Holmes—against whom Chesterton's fictional detective, Basil Grant, makes an insightful contrast.

---

31. Huxley, "Professor Huxley on Men of Science," *The Mechanics' Magazine*, 14 October 1871, 284-85.

TRUTH BEFORE LOGIC

In *The Club of Queer Trades*, Basil responds to his brother, Rupert, after examining evidence which ostensibly points to an attempted murder. He disagrees with his brother's conclusion about the guilt of the suspect, suggesting that there is more to consider than the facts alone:

> "I don't think it's the sort of letter one criminal would write to another." [said Basil]
> "My dear boy, you are glorious," cried Rupert . . . "Your methods amaze me. Why, there is the letter. It is written, and it does give orders for a crime . . ."
> "That's rather good," he said; "but, of course, logic like that's not what is really wanted. It's a question of spiritual atmosphere. It's not a criminal letter."
> "It is. It's a matter of fact," cried the other in an agony of reasonableness.
> "Facts," murmured Basil, like one mentioning some strange, far-off animal, "how facts obscure the truth."[32]

Rupert plays the part of the rigid logician and suffers an "agony of reasonableness" because he tries to get from logical deductions certain comprehensive truths they cannot give. The argument between Basil and Rupert is the narrative expression of the principle Chesterton explains in *Orthodoxy* in contrasting poets and mathematicians:

> Exactly what does breed insanity is reason. Poets do not go mad; but chess-players do. Mathematicians go mad, and cashiers; but creative artists very seldom. I am not, as will be seen, in any sense attacking logic: I only say that this danger does lie in logic, not in imagination.
> The general fact is simple. Poetry is sane because it floats easily in an infinite sea; reason seeks to cross the infinite sea, and so make it finite. The result is mental exhaustion . . . The poet only desires exaltation and expansion, a world to stretch himself in. The poet only asks to get his head into the heavens. It is the logician who

---

32. Chesterton, *The Club of Queer Trades*, 22

seeks to get the heavens into his head. And it is his head that splits.[33]

In Chesterton's view, the popular notion exemplified by Sherlock Holmes—that linear inferences from keenly observed empirical facts always lead to a full knowledge of the truth—is fundamentally misguided. He further expounds the importance of a wider horizon of knowledge in his criticism of Sherlock's creator, Sir Alfred Conan Doyle, regarding controversies over changes in marriage statutes in early twentieth-century England. In response to Doyle's comment that those who opposed changes in British marriage laws did so only because of "certain texts" in the Bible, Chesterton says belief in the binding nature of marriage, like the belief in the brotherhood of man, is "not hung on one text but on a hundred truths."[34] In the same vein he insists that "a man may well be less convinced of a philosophy from four books, than from one book, one battle, one landscape, and one old friend. The very fact that the things are of different kinds increases the importance of the fact that they all point to one conclusion."[35]

In Basil Grant's argument with his brother, he goes on to explain the problem:

> I never could believe in that man—what's his name, in those capital stories?—Sherlock Holmes. Every detail points to something, certainly; but generally to the wrong thing. Facts point in all directions, it seems to me, like the thousands of twigs on a tree. It's only the life of the tree that has unity and goes up—only the green blood that springs, like a fountain, at the stars.'[36]

The key point here is that "the life of the tree . . . has unity." To see a tree is to see a unified reality that is more than the sum of its material parts.[37] When the empirically accessible facts of a tree are

---

33. Chesterton, *Orthodoxy*, 21
34. Chesterton, *The Superstition of Divorce*
35. Chesterton, *Orthodoxy*, 150
36. ibid
37. "Tree" is a category of identity—a Platonic essence—and a person's

thought to be the only "real" parts, then one cannot see the full reality of the tree. The irony in this is that the value of scientism is thought to be in its accuracy of perception—"we just believe the facts"—when focusing on the factual at the expense of the conceptual actually makes one blind to the only meaningful reality in what is perceived. Rather than missing the forest for the trees, scientism makes it so that one cannot see the tree itself for the forest of its atomized, physical properties. To put the point more technically, it undermines the capacity for apperception,[38] which is the fundamental mode of human consciousness.

At a more fundamental level, the deficiency in scientism is its inability not only to properly account for objects of perception but also for the essence of the perceiver. A reflexive response to Chesterton's description of the life of a tree from a science-only mindset is to say that imagery of green blood and a fountain springing to the stars is "only" a subjective musing from the observer, that it is "only psychological," but psychological does not mean subjective or imaginary, as in "only in the mind." In the most literal sense, it means a characterization of the self (psyche).

Plant life is necessary in maintaining a healthy psychological state—that is, a healthy state of the self—because there is an aspect of the human soul[39] that resonates with, rather feeds upon, the ver-

---

awareness that an object with myriad branches and leaves stemming from a vertical trunk belongs in the category of "tree" rather than "lake" or "cloud" is a fundamental criterion of sanity. Also see Immanuel Kant's explanation of the "Transcendental unity of apperception." In neuroscience, the same concept is referred to as the "binding problem," which is the question of how the neurological processes of the brain can instantly perceive a unity upon perception—such as a man or a fir tree—rather than perceiving the tremendous multitude of individual parts and subsequently inferring that the parts comprise a unified whole.

38. Apperception refers to the unifying essence of perception. Though the physical objects that present to our senses are conglomerations of disparate matter, we see them as unified, distinct entities—as a tree, or my friend, Bob. Neuroscientists may refer to this as the "binding problem," as it poses the question of how the mind binds the multitude of perceived data points together to "see" or "recognize" a distinct, intelligible object.

39. The Greek word, "psyche," means "soul" or "self"

dant beauty of plant life. This is all the more clear in considering the opposite experience. One may dismiss the sense of barrenness as a subjective, psychological state, but to do so is to dismiss a fundamental reality about the human self. The concept of barrenness does not mean mitigated forest density resulting in a decrease in oxygen production from photosynthesis. It means a kind of lifelessness that is to the human soul what emaciation is to the body.

A purely scientific approach dismisses the kinds of musings that see in a tree "the green blood that springs, like a fountain, at the stars," as a fanciful, and therefore distorted, judgment about the nature of the tree. But the missed insight lies at a deeper level. To assume that an empirical knowledge of bark and leaves nullifies a psychological knowledge of verdancy and barrenness is to obscure the truth of what a tree is with the facts of its material composition. To assume that the human psychological experience of a tree is subjective and therefore insignificant—or that it is only a matter of brain function—is to obscure the truth of the human person with facts about human neurology. No matter what can or cannot be accurately said about the physical properties of the tree, it is a fact about the essence of human beings that we are incorrigibly prone to see something more than those physical properties.

CHAPTER 4

Beauty, Knowledge, and a Human Science that Excludes Humanity

> "The simplest truth about man is that he is a very strange being, almost in the sense of being a stranger on the earth. In all sobriety, he has much more of the external appearance of one bringing alien habits from another land than of a mere growth of this one."
>
> G.K. Chesterton, *The Everlasting Man*

THE MAIN IDEA IN Chesterton's *The Everlasting Man* is the spiritual essence of human beings. He begins by targeting the common caricature of a Cave-Man to refute the idea that human beings evolved from a bestial to an intellectually and aesthetically sophisticated nature by arguing that man is "everlasting." Human essence has been from its beginning something qualitatively different from the natural environment so that "the more we really look at man as an animal, the less he will look like one."[1] Humans have animal needs, but animals do not have human needs. Dogs and elephants have no need for art, or religion, or a sense of humor. People, however, simply *see* that color and music are good in themselves, that it makes sense to put candles on birthday cakes, and that one *should* stand to honor a flag. To understand the reasonableness of things

---

1. Chesterton, *The Everlasting Man*, 27

like these is to have a particular kind of knowledge, a knowledge of what Chesterton calls "the real things of the earth."[2] It is an understanding of the things which are most real but are not practical in nature and cannot be understood through scientific observation. They can only be known from the inside.

As in the explanation of knowledge that precedes proof in Chapter Two, this distinction is between practical knowledge gained from external observation and a distinctly human knowledge which comes in the conscious awareness of something. He clarifies the point in the way he explains his perception of the earth, "not by the hackneyed insistence of its relative position to the sun, but by some imaginative effort to conceive its remote position for the dehumanized spectator . . . I do not believe in being dehumanized in order to study humanity."[3] In this passage he clarifies the singular idea at the heart of his approach to truth-seeking and the fundamental flaw in scientism. Believing that the only knowable reality is that which is subject to direct observation and calculation is a dehumanizing belief because it denies the most fundamental kinds of human knowledge.

Along with our capacity for scientific observation and logical deduction, we are imaginative, aesthetic, intuitive, emotional, sensual, relational creatures, and a person is only able to know what something truly is when he is able to see the thing through all the lenses of these myriad aspects of human consciousness. In other words, the intellect is not the only aspect of a human being that enables us to discern what is true and real. Failing to appreciate this inevitably results in distorted, truncated perspective. An approach to understanding the earth, for example, relegated to a purely mathematical or astrophysical framework distorts our knowledge of the full essence of the earth much as it would distort our understanding of the works of Shakespeare if we believed their only value was in giving insight on the state of the English economy in the late sixteenth-century.

---

2. Chesterton, *Orthodoxy*, 27
3. Chesterton, *The Everlasting Man*, 23

In response to the notion that the earth's small size as a planet in relation to the rest of the cosmos is evidence of its ultimate insignificance, Chesterton insists, "that we do not even know that it is a planet at all, in the sense in which we know that it is a place; and a very extraordinary place too."[4] To know the earth as a planet is to know the number of miles between it and the sun and the ratio of carbon and oxygen molecules in its atmosphere. To know it as a place is to know the pristine solemnity that reverberates in the soul at the sound of moon-gilded Gulf of Mexico waves dissolving into the shore in symphonic crash. It is to know the surge of ecstatic severity and ennobling humility that comes with a hundred-mile vista from an alpine ridge. It is to know the particular bliss of the pizza sub one can only get at that place with the faded sign next to the laundromat at the corner of 25th and Lowry Lane. It is to know the inner warmth of autumn and the inner coolness of spring, the personality of a dog and the elegance of a cat. It is to understand what the poet, Seamus Heaney, meant when he described, "that moment when the bird sings very close to the music of what happens."[5]

Contrary to the negative connotations of the term "subjective," the subjectivity of experiential knowledge in no way diminishes its importance nor its status as genuine knowledge. Scientism blinds its devotees in obscuring the realities known through subjective experiences by appealing to mechanical theories about the experience. People in prescientific ages inferred incorrect scientific conclusions from their perception of spiritual realities. Modern adherents of scientism seek to remedy this by inferring incorrect conclusions about spiritual realities from their scientific understanding of the material world.

C.S. Lewis explains how a scientific over-correction of prescientific superstitions blinds us not only to the full reality of material objects but also to our very selves:

---

4. ibid
5. Seamus Heaney, "Song."

> The same method which has emptied the world now proceeds to empty ourselves. The masters of the method soon announce that we were just as mistaken (and mistaken in much the same way) when we attributed "souls", or "selves" or "minds" to human organisms, as when we attributed Dryads to the trees . . . Just as the Dryad is a "ghost", an abbreviated symbol for all the facts we know about the tree foolishly mistaken for a mysterious entity over and above the facts, so the man's "mind" or "consciousness" is an abbreviated symbol for certain verifiable facts about his behavior: a symbol mistaken for a thing.[6]

This passage homes in on the most basic problem with scientism. It is a human endeavor which excludes humanity. When a reasonable scientist realizes that the human self (that is, the soul—"psyche") cannot be observed and examined like the material properties of the body, he concludes that the self/soul is not completely comprised of matter. The devotee of scientism, on the other hand, concludes that the self must not exist because he is committed above all else to the notion that immaterial realities are impossible.

He is like a drunk man looking for his lost keys only within the small circle of sidewalk illuminated by a streetlight. When asked what makes him think the keys are lying within the scope of the light, he says, "They have to be there. That's the only place I can see."[7] As with fundamentalists of all kinds, disciples of scientism are so committed to the belief that their theory is comprehensive and immutable, facts that don't comport with the theory are denied, distorted, or ignored.

Lewis also vividly illustrates the psychologically destructive effects of scientific reductionism in his fictional account of the pilgrim, John, imprisoned by the Spirit of the Age in *The Pilgrim's Regress*. The scientific zeitgeist is personified by a giant whose "eyes had this property, that whatever they looked on became transparent." Because of this, John recoils in terror upon seeing the other prisoners in the dungeon as he sees not the people but their

---

6. Lewis, "The Empty Universe."
7. I first heard this analogy given in a talk by Alvin Plantinga.

disparate, bodily parts isolated from the full reality of the whole person:

> The place seemed to be thronged with demons. A woman was seated near him, but he did not know it was a woman because, through the face, he saw the skull and through that the brains and the passages of the nose, and the larynx, and the saliva moving in the glands and the blood in the veins . . . And when John sat down and drooped his head, not to see the horrors, he saw only the working of his own inwards . . . And John looked round on it all and suddenly he fell on his face and thrust his hands into his eyes and cried out . . . "I am mad. I am dead. I am in hell forever."[8]

When all value is placed on the scientific instruments of sight and not the value of the things seen, then the person can no longer see things but only see through them. The end result is a profound blindness. Primitive farmers winnowed their wheat crops to blow away the worthless chaff and keep the valuable grain. In denying everything beyond the scope of empirical observation, reductionistic scientists keep the chaff of tangible particles and blow away the grain of soul and truth.

Lewis explains this tragi-comic thinking error through Lady Reason, who liberates John from the zeitgeist dungeon and explains to him the realities screened out by the logical pathology of the spirit of the age:

> The warmth in your limbs at this moment, the sweetness of your breath as you draw it in, the comfort in your belly because we breakfasted well, and your hunger for the next meal—these are the reality; all the sponges and tubes that you saw in the dungeon are the lie.
>
> Is it surprising that things should look strange if you see them as they are not? If you take an organ out of a man's body—or a longing out of the dark part of a man's mind—and give to the one the shape and the color, and to the other the self-consciousness, which they never

---

8. Lewis, *The Pilgrim's Regress*, 47

have in reality, would you expect them to be other than monstrous?⁹

Indeed, conscious experiences "are the reality," and the way we understand the reality of something must be appropriate to the thing we're seeking to understand. This is why Chesterton says,

> In literature to be dispassionate is simply to be illiterate. To be disinterested is simply to be uninterested. The object of a book on comets, of course, is not to make us all feel like comets; but the object of a poem about warriors is to make us all feel like warriors. It is not merely true that the right method for one may be the wrong method for the other; it must be the wrong method for the other. A critic who takes a scientific view of the Book of Job is exactly like a surgeon who should take a poetical view of appendicitis.[10]

PRIMARY KNOWLEDGE

One of Chesterton's key insights which enables us to move beyond a short-sighted scientism to a sound and comprehensive *way* of knowing is the distinction between primary and secondary knowledge:

> In calling up this vision of the first things, I would ask the reader to make with me a sort of experiment in simplicity. And by simplicity I do not mean stupidity, but rather the sort of clarity that sees things like life rather than words like evolution...What we know, in a sense in which we know nothing else, is that the trees and the grass did grow and that a number of other extraordinary things do in fact happen . . . These are things and not theories; and compared with them evolution and the atom and even the solar system are merely theories.[11]

---

9. Lewis, *The Pilgrim's Regress*, 62
10. Chesterton, "Leviathan and the Hook," The Speaker, September 9, 1905
11. Chesterton, *The Everlasting Man*, 26

In making the distinction between seeing life and saying words like "evolution," the key point is the importance of first experiences ("first thoughts") which are "more clean, more just, more thankful, more comprehensive," and are "buried under a vast and star-kissing rubbish heap of deductions and generalisations."[12] As with Chesterton's example of the perception of the earth, the process of logical analysis should be subjugated to the experience of "first thoughts" because the primary experience is more perceptually pure. Though a process of deductive analysis naturally follows the act of initial perception, the process should never be allowed to obscure that which one understands by her "first thoughts" upon perception.

In the raw act of perceiving a dynamic world filled with vast complexity, one *sees* an extraordinary reality. Such a vivid world is what is there. In contrast, words like evolution describe theories, postulations, or calculations. Chesterton's point is not to question the theory as such but to make clear that the startling, fascinating, vigorous, intelligible life which we know by simply perceiving is something "we know, in a sense in which we know nothing else," and a theory comprised of deductions is a secondary knowledge, true as it may be.

Later in *The Everlasting Man*, he elaborates on this principle by explaining a common error of conflation that occurs when the boundary between primary and secondary life collapses:

> If a man lives alone in a straw hut in the middle of Tibet, he may be told that he is living in the Chinese Empire... But the curious thing is that in certain mental states he can feel much more certain about the Chinese Empire that he cannot see than about the straw hut that he can see. He has some strange magical juggle in his mind, by which his argument begins with the empire though his experience begins with the hut. Sometimes he goes mad and appears to be proving that a straw hut cannot exist in the domains of the Dragon Throne; that it is impossible for such a civilization as he enjoys to contain such a hovel

---

12. Chesterton, "The Philosophy of First Thoughts," *The Speaker*, September 14, 1901

as he inhabits. But his insanity arises from the intellectual slip of supposing that because China is a large and all-embracing hypothesis, therefore it is something more than a hypothesis.[13]

The "intellectual slip" is that of conflating theoretical knowledge with that of firsthand, conscious experience, so that one obscures the knowledge of a self-evident reality with a commitment to a hypothesis. When it comes to the belief in a purely material world, if there is no room in the hypothesis for humanity then so much the worse for humanity.

The more well established and pervasive the hypothesis—and the more extensive the inferential chain—the more vulnerable we are to forgetting that we are hypothesizing and inferring at all. Chesterton continues from the analogy of the Tibetan hut dweller to elaborate the point:

> [Modern people] seem to forget, for instance, that a man is not even certain of the Solar System as he is certain of the South Downs. The Solar System is a deduction, and doubtless a true deduction; but the point is that it is a very vast and far-reaching deduction and therefore he forgets that it is a deduction at all and treats it as a first principle . . . [he is] almost ready to contradict the sun if it does not fit into the solar system.[14]

The South Downs is an example of something which "is not a logical thing but a primary and direct experience, like a physical sense, like a religious vision."[15] This is a different kind of knowledge than that which comes through deduction, and Chesterton insists that the process of discerning the veracity of deductive knowledge must be regulated by knowledge that is "primary and direct."

---

13. Chesterton, *The Everlasting Man*, 73
14. Ibid.
15. ibid

BEAUTY BEFORE LOGIC

One of the most important instances of primary knowledge is beauty, and it's hard to cite a more comically tragic example of secondary theory screening out primary reality than Richard Dawkins' perspective on how and why beauty is perceived. Dawkins is a highly intelligent man with a knowledge of the biological sciences one would expect in an Oxford professor and the philosophical acumen one would expect in a junior college freshman. He begins the eighth chapter of *Climbing Mount Improbable* with the following passage:

> I was driving through the English countryside with my daughter Juliet, then aged six, and she pointed out some flowers by the wayside. I asked her what she thought wildflowers were for. She gave a rather thoughtful answer: "Two things," she said. "To make the world pretty, and to help the bees make honey for us." I was touched by this and sorry I had to tell her that it wasn't true.[16]

This is a telling passage because a six-year-old girl does not immediately appeal to a theory. She simply sees that flowers are pretty. Then, like a stiff-lipped schoolmarm, Dawkins screens out the beauty the girl sees because it doesn't comport with his theory. In this case, an uneducated child understands something that her highly intelligent and academically renowned father cannot. Chesterton says about the power and function of images and symbols that, "everything that is pictorial suggests, without naming or defining. There is a road from the eye to the heart that does not go through the intellect."[17] But for those like Dawkins who are blinkered by scientism, there is only one road. The intricacies of the towns and the terrain not immediately visible from the freeway of the intellect are simply not seen.

The reference to flowers and one's blindness to their obvious beauty is especially striking in light of Chesterton's critique of a certain kind of blindness in George Bernard Shaw:

---

16. Dawkins, *Climbing Mount Improbable*, 256
17. Chesterton, *The Defendant*, "A Defense of Heraldry."

> Mr. Shaw, [has] been infected to some extent with the primary intellectual weakness of his new master, Nietzsche, the strange notion that the greater and stronger a man was the more he would despise other things. The greater and stronger a man is the more he would be inclined to prostrate himself before a periwinkle.[18]

That which constitutes greatness and strength is a clear moral and aesthetic faculty of perception which enables a person to see the true nature of things, a point he makes explicit in another critique of Shaw: "For the truth is Mr. Shaw has never seen things as they really are. If he had he would have fallen on his knees before them. He has always had a secret ideal that has withered all the things of this world."[19] Likewise, a world-withering ideal is a very apt description of the naturalist philosophy that blinds Dawkins to the beauty of flowers.

Just a few paragraphs later, Dawkins goes on to explain, "We must learn to see things through non-human eyes. In the case of the flowers with which we began our discussion, it is at least marginally more sensible to see them through the eyes of bees and other creatures that pollinate them."[20] Brief reflection on this causes more than a little dissonance. What are the implications of learning to "see things through non-human eyes"? If it's the case that we humans should learn to see all things in a non-human way, then who or what will be doing the seeing? How do we set aside our humanness in order to see things as bees do? Was he actually encouraging his daughter to think more like an insect than a human girl?

One also wonders how we might study in the humanities through non-human eyes? And how exactly should we understand inhumane behavior? The fact that Dawkins has been one of the loudest and most indignant critics of those scientifically ignorant enough to continue believing in supernatural realities also raises the question of how we are to understand, through non-human

18. Chesterton, *Heretics*, 26

19. ibid

20. Dawkins, *Climbing Mount Improbable*, 258

eyes, our moral obligation to align our beliefs with the facts of science rather than the superstition of religion?

The obvious reality which Dawkins and so many others have screened out by their pre-established beliefs is that "non-human eyes" do not see any value in science or religion. Most of the non-humans roaming the planet feel no impulse to encourage others to embrace one instead of the other. If, in fact, all people were so enlightened as to see everything through non-human eyes, Dawkins would likely never have been a prestigious professor as he would have been enslaved or eaten long ago by someone much stronger or more cunning than himself.

Writing in the generation after Chesterton and before Dawkins, the Hungarian chemist-turned-philosopher, Michael Polanyi, anticipated this kind of soulless scientism and the absurdities it produces:

> if we decided to examine the universe objectively in the sense of paying equal attention to portions of equal mass...not in a thousand million lifetimes would the turn come to give man even a second's notice. It goes without saying that no one—scientists included—looks at the universe this way, whatever lip-service is given to "objectivity."
>
> For, as human beings, we must inevitably see the universe from a center lying within ourselves and speak about it in terms of a human language shaped by the exigencies of human intercourse. Any attempt rigorously to eliminate our human perspective from our picture of the world must lead to absurdity.[21]

Polonyi's criticism echoes Chesterton's point that,

> The same frigid and detached spirit which leads to success in the study of astronomy or botany leads to disaster in the study of mythology or human origins. It is necessary to cease to be a man in order to do justice to a microbe; it is not necessary to cease to be a man in order to do justice to men. That same suppression of sympathies,

---

21. Polanyi, *Personal Knowledge*, pg. 3

> that same waving away of intuitions or guess-work which make a man preternaturally clever in dealing with the stomach of a spider, will make him preternaturally stupid in dealing with the heart of man. He is making himself inhuman in order to understand humanity.[22]

The tragedy in Dawkins' attempt to relegate knowledge to what can be seen with "non-human," purely intellectual eyes becomes poignantly clear when one realizes the exquisite realities missed by such a view. A personal experience comes to mind as a clear illustration of the kind of knowledge forfeited by naturalist philosophy.

One early November morning, I was hiking on an Alpine trail in central Utah.[23] A storm had passed through the night before leaving large swaths of clouds low in the valley but a pristine blue sky above. The view on the lower section of the trail was obscured by forest, but after gaining elevation, a sharp turn suddenly opened a fifty-mile vista. Instantly I was looking over a lake of clouds rimmed by green and granite ridges all under the light of a jewel blue sky. This was an aesthetic shock which struck the soul like a live wire strikes the body. It was, in Chesterton's words, "not a logical thing but a primary and direct experience . . . like a religious vision."[24] My eyes suddenly and unexpectedly welled with tears, and in that moment—in the immediate, uncalculated consciousness of what was before me—I *knew* something. That which I knew was lucid, distinct, and tremendously important, but also beyond the scope of clear logical explanation. That which is known in beauty cannot be clearly articulated because its full reality exceeds the capacity of verbal speech, but our inability to describe it with logical clarity in no way diminishes its significance. As Polanyi says, "We can know more than we can tell."[25]

Beauty is the thing seen not the theory thought. The experience of beauty is simultaneously like an electrical charge and a conduit through which a certain kind of electricity flows; the

---

22. Chesterton, *Heretics*, 60
23. Loafer Mountain
24. Chesterton, *The Everlasting Man*, 73
25. Michael Polanyi, *The Tacit Dimension*, 4

beautiful object is an object of knowledge in itself and a harbinger of a greater reality which imbues it with significance.[26] To truly see something beautiful is to see something of immense, objective value which hums and glows with the glory of a reality far beyond it. When one contemplates the question, "What exactly is going on when I am enamored by something beautiful?" it becomes evident that there is something distinct from one's self and objectively real which is known in the perception of profound beauty. In the bliss evoked at the sight, sound, and scent of an aspen grove in full autumn color, for example, there is a particular knowledge about something of which the glowing, yellow aspens are a messenger.

An awareness of the gestalt of one's surroundings is an awareness of a reality which gives a house, a city, or an aspen grove its unique character—a character which is distinct from the material parts through which the experience comes. The clear-headed thinkers Chesterton calls, "fairy tale philosophers," see that "every color has in it a bold quality as of choice; the red of garden roses is not only decisive but dramatic, like suddenly spilt blood. [They feel] that something has been done."[27]

This makes sense because meaningfulness necessarily implies intent; for something to be purposeful it must have been done "on purpose." Beauty, by definition, is meaningful and, therefore, intentional. This is not metaphysical speculation; it is just the raw data of human experience. Perceiving a meaningful reality in and through beautiful objects is just what it's like to experience beauty.

The fact that beauty is a conduit of transcendence is clear in the experience of elation, which is something like what one feels when he is struggling for the words to explain something of great importance and then hears another articulate the idea with perfect felicity. The natural response is, "Yes! That's it exactly! That's what I was trying to say!" Elation is different from mere sensual pleasure. It is a kind of affirmation; words that appropriately express the

---

26. For a nuanced explanation of the relationship between beauty, knowledge, and transcendent reality, see Chapter 4 of *The Soul's Upward Yearning*, by Robert Spitzer.

27. Chesterton, *Orthodoxy*, 64

sense of elation that comes in response to suddenly seeing exquisite beauty are "Yes!" "Right!" "So good!" And the emphatic "Yes!" is a yes in affirmation *of something*. Though we cannot articulate exactly what it is that beauty shows us, there is a clear knowledge in the soul that what engages us through beauty is substantial and good and should be welcomed and celebrated.

The art critic, Roger Fry, gives a lucid explanation of the nature of the experience:

> One can only say that those who experience [beauty] feel it to have a peculiar quality of "*reality*" which makes it a matter of infinite importance in their lives. Any attempt I might make to explain this would probably land me in the depths of mysticism. On the edge of that gulf I stop.[28]

A paradox of beauty is that it makes for a mystical experience, but the mystical realm it makes us aware of has "a peculiar quality of 'reality.'" We cannot give a clear explanation of that which enamors the soul through beauty other than to say that it is distinct, substantial, meaningful, and real. Also, it's most accurate to say beauty moves us *toward* a mystical reality, because one of its distinct characteristics is to cause immense but unsatisfied pleasure. As with a hungry person smelling food on a grill, there is a pleasure in the experience itself, but the immediate pleasure has no power to consummate the basic desire; the scent itself does not satisfy the hunger. The food which truly satisfies is that of which the smell is a harbinger. Likewise, beauty is always desirable, but experiencing it evokes a more intense desire. When a person is enamored with the beautiful, there is a magnetism—a sense of being drawn into or united with something that will consummate the desire kindled by the experience—but the experience itself never brings us fully to the point of consummation. Beauty is the scent of the transcendent reality for which the soul hungers.

That Something which beauty moves us toward cannot be accessed with the scientific method for the same reason a knowledge

---

28. Roger Fry, "Retrospect," in *Vision and Design*, ed. J.B. Bullen (Dover Publications, 1998) pg. 211 (Cited in *The Soul's Upward Yearning*, by Robert Spitzer, pg. 154)

of a person's character cannot be accessed with a blood test. Biomechanical explanations can be given, but they are inadequate because neurons and synapses alone do not comport with the true nature of what is observed. Brain activity is the effect not the cause. Believing that neurophysiology can explain the elation and desire for consummation which is the very essence of the experience of beauty is like believing that Rembrandt produced art by the same process that Rembrandt's pancreas produced insulin. To obscure or marginalize such profound knowledge because it cannot be explained with the scientific method is a deep tragedy, like an accountant who discards a love letter from a beautiful woman because it arrives in an over-sized envelope which doesn't fit neatly into the filer on his desk.

CHAPTER 5

The Human Mind Made for Myth

"The mythological imagination moves as it were in circles, hovering either to find a place or to return to it. In a word, mythology is a *search*."

G. K. Chesterton, *The Everlasting Man*

WOVEN THROUGHOUT CHESTERTON'S VAST body of work is an insight which is to the pursuit of wisdom what nutrition and exercise are to the pursuit of health. In the passage from *The Superstition of Divorce* cited in Chapter One, he says the problem with those who wanted to reform British marriage laws in the early twentieth century was that "They do the work that's nearest; which is poking holes in the bottom of a boat under the impression that they are digging in a garden."[1] This kind of Quixotic destruction happens when a concern for process and method eclipses the more important concerns of essence and meaning.

The problem with the science-only approach to knowledge is that it obscures the primary question of what a thing is by focusing on the secondary question of what a thing does, particularly when the thing in question is a human being. One of the most clear and consequential evidences of this is the pervasive misunderstanding of the nature of myth. The fact that the word has come to be a common synonym for empty fables or ignorant superstitions is

1. Chesterton, *The Superstition of Divorce*, Chapter 1.

evidence of the blinders placed on the contemporary mind by the enthronement of the empirical sciences. Scientists like those referenced earlier are prone to dismiss mythical stories as nonfactual and therefore false, bypassing the more fundamental and fascinating question of why myths have such a power to capture human attention, ignite imagination, and galvanize allegiance to a group or cause. They fail to consider the nature of the mind in which mythical stories so deeply resonate.

The fact that we can't travel to Gondor or that no one ever had dinner with Helen of Troy or Princess Lea suggests to the myopically scientific mind that such tales are fake stories whose only purpose is "escapism" or mindless amusement. This misses the paramount point that human beings are myth-making machines. An inability to understand myth is an inability to understand one of the most basic aspects of human nature and the most meaningful aspects of human experience, so that "he who has no sympathy with myth has no sympathy with men."[2]

The often unnoticed problem with this mindset is that it assumes people are, at our most basic level, only data gatherers. It reflects a fundamentally mechanical concept of human beings which believes observation, calculation, and practical application to be our central purpose for existence. But these scientific pursuits alone never motivate people at a deep level unless they take place in the context of a mythical story. Many scientists, for example, take pride in their commitment to the unbiased pursuit of truth. They conceive of themselves as light bearers, dispelling the fog of religious superstitions with the illumination of the scientific method—knights who answer the call to pursue the truth no matter how far from the status quo it may lead.

Some scientists lead people into the light of truth. Others lead in the opposite direction. In either case, the scientist is motivated by something far more important than the observation of facts. The endeavor of scientific inquiry is meaningful because it has a purpose; it is *about* something that matters, and its purpose is understood within the matrix of a narrative framework, such

---

2. Chesterton, *The Everlasting Man*, 109

The Human Mind Made for Myth

as liberating the world from oppressive superstition, or creating technology that will vanquish the evil of suffering and bring about the triumph of human flourishing. Without these kinds of moral narratives, the endeavor of science would have never begun. Man does not live by data alone.

What the Chesterton scholar, John Coates, says about literary and religious judgments is equally true about science:

> At the very heart of Chesterton's apologetic writing lies the conception of the story intuited through man's myth-making faculty and finally fulfilled. Behind both the literary and religious judgments lies the second and related assumption of life having the configuration, the proportions or structure of a story, being *like* a story in its texture, rather than like a theory or a logical sequence.[3]

It doesn't occur to those committed to a science-only worldview to ask what should be inferred from that fact that human beings are incorrigibly imaginative creatures who think in narrative terms. It's easy to argue that dryads aren't real, but it is philosophically lazy to treat such an obvious point as the end of the matter without considering the significance of the fact that dryads are imagined by real minds which have an implacable instinct for perceiving a reality of which dryads are emblematic.

Myths are not factual but it is an obvious fact that we are moved by them. This is plain, straightforward anthropology, and the part of us to which myths are both intelligible and compelling is more basic than the calculating intellect which marginalizes myths when it operates independently of the other faculties or senses which should inform it. This being the case, those who try to explain everything in terms of what can be observed, quantified, and calculated are like a small boy Chesterton describes who, being annoyed by a violent windstorm, asks his mother, "Why don't you take away the trees, and then [the wind would stop]."[4] When it comes to the most meaningful aspects of life, those who put their faith in nothing but science constantly mistake effects for causes.

3. Coates, *Chesterton and The Edwardian Cultural Crisis*, 145
4. Chesterton, *Tremendous Trifles*, "The Wind and the Trees," 60-61

They mistake the trees for the wind. He goes on to explain that the boy who mistakenly thought the trees were the cause of the wind was,

> very like the principal modern thinkers, only much nicer . . . the trees stand for all visible things and the wind for the invisible. The wind is the spirit which bloweth where it listeth; the trees are the material things of the world which are blown where the spirit lists. The wind is philosophy, religion, revolution; the trees are cities and civilizations.[5]

He appeals to the same principle in criticizing a naturalistic explanation of the development of religion. Just as the moral obligation to prioritize the pursuit of knowledge and truth for their own sake is preliminary to scientific study, a perception of religious significance in aspects of the natural world is preliminary to the development of religious beliefs. Scientific study itself cannot explain the human passion and conviction that drives it, and the natural phenomena often cited in explaining the development of religious beliefs could not create such beliefs without a religious sensibility already present in the mind of those who believe:

> In other words, it is hardly an adequate explanation of how a thing appeared for the first time to say it existed already. Similarly, we cannot say that religion arose out of the religious forms, because that is only another way of saying that it only arose when it existed already. It needed a certain sort of mind to see that there was anything mystical about the dreams or the dead, as it needed a particular sort of mind to see that there was anything poetical about the skylark or the spring. That mind was presumably what we call the human mind, very much as it exists to this day.[6]

If people were, at their core, only data gatherers—matter-of-fact observers, conscious without a conscience—then no matter how many objects are observed, a person would never be moved to

---

5. ibid
6. Chesterton, *The Everlasting Man*, 48

arrange them in the form of an altar nor to catalogue and classify them for the advancement of science. There would be no dangerous experiments in search of a breakthrough in medicine or machinery.

The very concept of "breakthrough" clarifies the point. Breakthrough implies the breaching of a barrier impeding progress. One must have a clear notion of an ideal state in order to perceive a barrier which must be broken through to get to that ideal. If all there is is data gathering people in a purely material world, then there is only one way of existing; all things simply are as they are. But if that's true, there would be nothing to break through. Since there is only the material world, there would be no better world to break through *to*. One can attribute the motive of defeating disease and natural disaster to "survival instinct," but that doesn't account for the heroism and sense of victory intrinsic in the notion of breakthrough. There is nothing in survival instinct that makes us proud of the virtues that enable us to survive.

In a purely material world there would be no endeavors or explorations across wild frontiers. The impetus for exploration is in the explorer not in the explored. "It will be hard to maintain that the Arctic explorers went north with the same material motive that made the swallows go south. And if you leave things like all the religious wars and all the merely adventurous explorations out of the human story, it will not only cease to be human at all but cease to be a story at all."[7] An explorer embarking on an endeavor in search of a breakthrough is a storyline because the concepts of exploration, endeavor, and breakthrough are distinctively narrative concepts. These words are unintelligible apart from a perceived value in knowledge for its own sake and of the importance of the virtues of commitment and fortitude often necessary to gain access to previously hidden facts *for the sake of* human progress toward an acknowledged ideal state. To simply observe is not an endeavor. A polar bear traversing large swaths of arctic ice fields in search of a plump seal is not exploring. A bird is not honored by

---

7. Chesterton, *The Everlasting Man*, 137

other birds for her intrepid navigation skills when she returns to the same point of migratory origin after a 2,000 mile round trip.

This is one of the most fundamental and important facts of anthropology obscured by scientism. People are in awe at the exquisite precision of birds' migratory patterns and by the sophisticated, instinctual intelligence by which they build their nests. But birds are not in awe of the sophisticated machines people have created to enable them to join birds in flight. There is no evidence that birds furnish their nests with pillows embroidered with images of humans. Birds don't have human mascots. American birds don't choose favored groups of people as their designated state human. This is so because birds, like all animals, operate by instinct and intelligence but not imagination. Mysticism and narrative are not only distinctly human interests but the distinctly human way of thinking. We see the mystical beauty in birds because we have an inherent mystical sensibility. C.S. Lewis' explanation of the uniquely human experience of awe at the size of the universe is much to the point:

> For light years and geological periods are mere arithmetic until the shadow of man, the poet, the maker of myths, falls upon them. As a Christian I do not say we are wrong to tremble at that shadow, for I believe it to be the shadow of an image of God. But if the vastness of Nature ever threatens to overcrow our spirits, we must remember that it is only Nature spiritualized by human imagination which does so.[8]

Nature is spiritualized and science is ennobled by the human imagination specifically because people are inherently imaginative creatures, and because the capacity for imagination enables a person to *see* something in (or through) the natural world that is not accessible to the empirical senses alone. Otherwise, the most awe-inspiring aspects of the universe are "mere arithmetic."

To be in awe of the night sky or the vastness of the Grand Canyon is to be aware of something real in the greatest sense of the word. The experience of awe is the experience of being *under*

8. C.S. Lewis, *Miracles*, 73

The Human Mind Made for Myth

Something profoundly real, and it is that soul-shaking, sehnsucht-evoking[9] Something that a rigid scientism screens out. There is no place in the science-only worldview for the "certain sort of mind" which is awed by the size of the universe, or which sees, "anything poetical about the skylark or the spring." Like it or not, human beings are conscious, willful, spiritual creatures. Mythical and religious sensibility is often thought to be the opposite of logical thinking and scientific inquiry, but the orientation of mind that makes myth intelligible is also that which understands logical integrity as moral and science as wonderful. The yearning, mystical, blazing human spirit is the force of internal combustion that moves the engines of logic and science.

MYTH AS A MEANS OF FINDING TRUTH

Whether in science or any other meaningful endeavor, we conceptualize our experiences as aspects of an unfolding story by intellectual instinct much like a lion conceptualizes a gazelle as food by physiological instinct. Lions, in particular, make for an apt illustration. A lion is known to people as "king" of the jungle because the human mind automatically conceives of animals as having a place in a particular narrative scheme in which it makes sense that lions reign over a kingdom, or that snakes are stealthy and threatening. To say that these are imaginary notions imposed on an amoral, purely biological world is to miss the point.

Aside from the question of whether the regality of lions or the furtiveness of snakes are actually inherent qualities, it is the inherent nature of the human mind to conceive of the animal kingdom in this way. It is natural to think of it as a *kingdom* and unnatural to think of it as sets of zoological categories. We naturally think in terms of a dynamic, narrative scheme in which there is nobility, power, order and the threat of usurping subterfuge. Myth is a mode of cognition because cognizing experiences in terms of a purposeful, ordered, story is a fundamental aspect of human

---

9. Sehnsucht: a German word for deep, inarticulate longing—intense yearning—conceptually similar to the Portuguese word "Saudade."

thinking. Failure to understand this is a failure to understand anthropology at the most basic level.

When myth is understood as a sense-making narrative, it becomes clear that it is the basic language of thought. It is the software code precisely formatted to the operating system of the mind.[10] An instinctual proneness to make sense of the world in terms of grand stories of lost loves regained, of victory against overwhelming odds, of goodness and order conquering evil and chaos—is an irreducible aspect of human thinking. This may sound like a controversial claim, but our everyday conscious experiences are saturated with demonstrable evidence. For example, six of the top grossing film series in our scientifically enlightened, superstition-free age are Avatar, Star Wars, Avengers, Spider Man, Harry Potter, and Lord of the Rings. Hundreds of millions of people across the world have been drawn to these stories comprised of characters, events, and places that do not exist in any empirically observable way, and yet people are captivated by them because there is something in these stories that resonates deeply with the human mind.

Though hobbits aren't physically real, when the story is told of Sam and Frodo and friends enduring an arduous journey and vanquishing evil by carrying the ring to Mordor despite their own inner weaknesses and the disproportionate force wielded by their sinister enemy, there is something inside a person with which that story resonates. There is a consciousness, a sense, a capacity of understanding primary to any logical calculation that says "Yes. Of course. This is how things 'should' be. This is right. This is keeping with the nature of how ultimate reality truly is."

There is meaning in the story because the story reflects the things that we already know give life meaning. The story moves and captivates people at a deep level because in hearing it we are reminded of what our lives really should be about. The climactic moment when the ring is finally dissolved in Mount Doom is only gratifying to a person (to the hundreds of millions of people who

---

10. The author realizes the irony of analogizing the human mind with a computer while arguing for the spiritual, non-mechanical essence of human beings.

have been so taken with the story) who has an intuitive understanding that victory is not determined by appearances, that good and evil are fundamental realities, and that our commitment to virtues like friendship and courage and our struggles against our own inner weaknesses are tremendously consequential.

This is why there will never be a blockbuster movie whose plot consists only of a man getting a job at a large corporation which provides him with a net income in excess of his monthly expenses, adequate medical insurance, and a 401K to pay off his mortgage the day before retirement at age 65. The end. In the wake of such a film, there will be no lucrative merchandise—no action figures that come with financial statements "just like in the movie"—no T-shirts or bumper stickers emblazoned with a silhouette of the protagonist and the words "401K all the way!" Images of the tree of Gondor or the Captain America shield will never be replaced by that of a briefcase and a balance sheet. Practicality does not inspire. Pragmatism will never be heroism because there is nothing in the depths of the human heart that resonates with pure pragmatism; there is nowhere in the soul for a purely pragmatic story to land.

As Chesterton puts it,

> The pragmatist tells a man to think what he must think and never mind the Absolute. But precisely one of the things that he must think is the Absolute. This philosophy, indeed, is a kind of verbal paradox. Pragmatism is a matter of human needs; and one of the first of human needs is to be something more than a pragmatist.[11]

The inspiration we feel from mythical stories, ideas, or objects is much like the warmth we feel from a heavy coat in cold weather. The coat itself doesn't warm us. A cadaver will remain the same temperature with or without one. Along with shielding from wind and weather, a coat traps the heat already present in the body. Likewise, mythical stories help to shield us from the deadening winds of secular pragmatism by stoking and maintaining the fire of transcendence already present in the soul. The chief evidence

---

11. Chesterton, *Orthodoxy*, 41-42

of this is the sheer ubiquity of myth. Without an inner sense of the transcendent, mythical stories would never become culture-shaping, blockbuster books and films. They would be senseless and have no place in our conscious life.

The power of myth also shows that the intelligibility of certain concepts is distinct from and primary to their empirical verifiability. Mythical stories resonate deep in the consciousness despite the fact that they are beyond the perceived boundaries of possibility established by our practical experiences. In other words, a wide range of mythical stories and concepts are made intelligible by a pre-logical orientation of mind so that myths are intelligible without being empirically accessible. A passage from *The Everlasting Man* illuminates the point:

> Suppose somebody in a story says "Pluck this flower and a princess will die in a castle beyond the sea," we do not know why something stirs in the subconsciousness, or why what is impossible seems almost inevitable. Suppose we read "And in the hour when the king extinguished the candle his ships were wrecked far away on the coast of Hebrides." We do not know why the imagination has accepted that image before the reason can reject it; or why such correspondences seem really to correspond to something in the soul.[12]

The imagination accepts certain fantastic images and events "before the reason can reject it" because imagination is distinct from and primary to our capacity for calculative reason. Imagination is more than a means of extrapolating from past experiences or an amusing fantasy generator. It is also a faculty of cognition, though not one which enables a person to acquire new knowledge from a state of ignorance like a trade apprentice or a student of chemistry. This is why Chesterton says,

> The student cannot make a scientific statement about the [savage's myth], because the savage is not making a scientific statement about the world. He is saying something quite different; what might be called the gossip of

12. Chesterton, *The Everlasting Man*, 105

the gods. We may say, if we like, that it is believed before there is time to examine it. It would be truer to say it is accepted before there is time to believe it.[13]

MYTHS, THE REMEDY FOR SPIRITUAL AMNESIA

Mythical stories and symbols enable us to recognize (that is, re-cognize, or cognize *again*) certain realities much like a recovering amnesiac recognizes the identity of formally familiar friends and places. The amnesiac may not be able to say where or how he knows the one speaking to him. He may not remember the person's name, but something registers. The face and the voice are familiar, though without an awareness of the logical connections that clarify how and when the relationship was established. There is a nebulous-but-certain sense that, "I know this person. She is not new to me."

In a similar way, mythical stories have a mysterious intelligibility. If the amnesiac is pressed to give a logically cogent explanation of how he knows his interlocutor, if he is asked to "prove" that she really is a close friend, he will not be able to do so. And yet, his interaction with her confirms in a place deep within his consciousness that he does know her. In much the same way, one is not likely to give a satisfactory answer to a rigid logician who demands a clear explanation of how a story of a young boy killing a flying dragon makes any sense when we know that flying dragons don't exist. And yet, such stories do resonate in a deep way with a vast number of people. There is something in them that makes sense in a distinct way.

That element in one's consciousness with which myth resonates is a particular kind of knowledge. A person resonates with a story because the story articulates a certain truth the person already knows but cannot tell. As when one stands on the shore, weak-kneed at the sight of the colossal, crashing blue majesty of the ocean, to be moved by a myth is to be confronted with a

---

13. Chesterton, *The Everlasting Man*, 103

powerful reality. The confrontation takes place between the reality portrayed in the story and the inchoate awareness of it within the human consciousness.

To put it differently, profound truths about ultimate realities are accessed through myths just as the profound reality of a human being is accessed through a phone. There is no physical part of the phone or the cell tower that *contains* the person who is speaking. In a purely physical sense, the person heard through th phone is a myth. If the phone is all there is, then the person on the line doesn't actually exist. In hearing the representation of the voice through the phone, however, we do engage with a real person.[14] A person's voice comes not *from* but *through* the phone. In much the same way, truths about the ultimately Real come though the places and characters in mythical stories though they are not physically real. Like beauty, myth is a conduit of Reality.

This being the case, it is almost comically facile to congratulate ourselves for learning that dryads can't be caught and classified like horses (this would not be news to many ancient people). Myths are powerful because they are the mental equivalents of a map of the cosmos. Like a painting of the solar system, myths give us easily perceptible pictures which correlate to a grand reality too vast to be seen and understood within the framework of our very limited senses. The power in the picture is in the awareness that it is not abstract. A painting of the solar system captures our attention because we know it correlates with real planets and moons. Likewise, the human mind is incorrigibly captivated by mythical stories because of a deep sense that those stories are indicative of something that is truly real.

> . . . imaginative does not mean imaginary. It does not follow that it is all what the moderns call subjective, when they mean false. Every true artist does feel, consciously or unconsciously, that he is touching transcendental truths; that his images are shadows of things seen through the veil. In other words, the natural mystic does know that

---

14. For a more developed form of this argument, see the essay, "Behind the Scenes" by C.S. Lewis.

there is something there; something behind the clouds or within the trees; but he believes that the pursuit of beauty is the way to find it; that imagination is a sort of incantation that can call it up.[15]

Artists, along with the bulk of humanity who lived before the moon of empiricism eclipsed the sun of transcendence, *see* a reality reflected in the natural world. Therefore, it is fundamentally at odds with the facts of human nature to believe that there is no reality beyond the natural world. This would be like acknowledging the existence of telescopes and denying the existence of stars.

---

15. Chesterton, *The Everlasting Man*, pg. 105

CHAPTER 6

The Squib and the Stained Glass

> "It is, perhaps, the strongest mark of the divinity of man that he talks of this world as 'a strange world,' though he has seen no other."
>
> Stanley Jaki, *Chesterton Seer of Science*

A FRIEND ONCE TOLD me of an elderly lady riding in her younger family member's car when GPS phone apps were still new. After listening to the voice give directions from the driver's iPhone, the baffled woman asked if there was a tower close by from which the woman speaking through the phone was watching their car. How else, she wondered, could that person possibly know where they were going? Much like that elderly woman, those who believe that human consciousness, aesthetic experience, and moral convictions can be explained purely in terms of synapses and neurochemicals are comically naïve because of their inability to acknowledge realities not immediately present to the senses.

Everywhere and always, our immediate, physical experiences are meaningful only because of a reality which transcends them. This is not a new insight. Augustine wrote over sixteen hundred years ago of the relationship between the natural world and that reality which is the source and consummation of the beauty we perceive in it, namely God: "But what is it that I love? I asked the earth, and it said, 'It's not me,' and everything in it admitted the same thing. I asked the sea and the great chasms of the deep, and the creeping things that have the breath of life in them, and they answered, 'We aren't your God: search above us.'"[1]

The yearning to "search above" highlights the facilitating nature of the material world and the necessity of the transcendent reality which imbues and illuminates it. From where does the joy of reuniting with a long-absent loved one originate? In the sound waves of his voice travelling through the airport corridor? In the tissues of his vocal chords? In the cochlea and auditory nerves in your inner ear? No. Search above. It's the person who is the source. The airport and the eardrum are preciously valuable because they facilitate the presence of the person.

Aside from any formal argument, this is evident in the commonplace ways we distinguish value in material objects. The rock lying next to the sidewalk outside my office window, for example, is meaningless. If it were taken away or destroyed, I wouldn't care. But the rock sitting on my bookshelf is very meaningful because I picked it up on a hike in a majestic canyon with a close friend. The rock in the office could consist of the same kind of material as the one on the sidewalk, but the one on the shelf has value because of the immaterial realities of which it was a part. It is valuable because it was an element in experiencing the beauty of opulent sandstone cathedrals under a blue and white dappled sky, and because it was part of a shared experience with a friend.

Like bits of asteroid found in the earth's surface, the rock on my shelf is a tangible link to another world—a world that resonates with the deepest, most significant parts of me. Exquisite, desert rock towers rising under a vast western sky are more conducive to the life of the soul than the off-white drywall and beige carpet in my office. As the moon is illuminated by the sun, the rock on my shelf is illuminated, in a sense, with the beauty of the canyon. The rock also evokes a longing to return to the canyon, but if I were to do so I would find that the canyon itself is imbued with a mysterious incandescence from beyond it.

---

1. Augustine, *Confessions*, 284

It would be easy for many who've consistently breathed the reductionistic fumes of scientism to dismiss this kind of value as "just" sentimental. But valuing scientific insight for its propensity to triumph over superstition and credulity is just as much a sentiment. Regardless of whether our understanding of the meaning of something is ill-founded or misguided, matter can only ever be a conduit, token, or embodiment of meaning. The sense of triumph in discovering a chemical relationship that cures cancer is not produced by chemical relationships, and the hormones at work in the reproductive system do not produce the love that moves a couple to marry and conceive a child. Material objects *facilitate* a kind of communication with a reality which transcends them.[2] Whether a small rock from an ethereal landscape, a tattered stuffed animal recovered from a dusty attic, a football jersey, or a wedding ring, tangible objects emit a radio frequency broadcasted from a country many miles from the isolation of our empirical island.

Our attention is drawn to a beautiful painting, for example, but it is an obvious absurdity to think that someone with a powerful microscope could locate the beauty in the chemical bonds of the oil pigments. Those pigments, the painting they comprise, and every other material object of any importance has a place in a matrix of meaning in which matter becomes the material component or vehicle of love or heartbreak, elation or frustration, victory or defeat. Just as the node connecting segments of rope in a net has no function and no importance if it is plucked from the net and set by itself, matter conceived in isolation from its place as the facilitating medium for acts of the human will is meaningless.

It should also be kept in mind that the meaning of tangible objects being dependent on an intangible reality should make us less prone to drive a wedge between the two. The perpetually dissecting, Cartesian[3] mind is prone to compartmentalize the various

---

2. The concept I have in mind here is the same basic principle as the ancient doctrine of metaphysical "participation"—that matter has intelligible shape and function because it participates in, or is ordered by, an immaterial form, and the forms of all things originate in the mind of God.

3. The French philosopher and mathematician, Rene Descartes, is known for his dualistic philosophy which proposes a distinct separation between

aspects of an experience by setting the material parts on one side and the transcendent parts on the other, but this way of thinking too easily leads us to a cold and distorted reductionism. Though it is true that material objects get their significance from a reality that transcends them, they are taken up into, or infused with that reality so that they become inseparable aspects of it, as with the power that heats and illuminates a red-hot piece of iron. The heat is not generated by the iron, but it is taken into or infuses the iron so that heat and luminosity actually become qualities of the iron and it becomes part of the fire.

C.S. Lewis' interplanetary protagonist, Dr. Ransom, puts the point in clear light as he reflects on a common, scientifically misguided mode of thought:

> The distinction between natural and supernatural, in fact, broke down; and where it had done so, one realized how great a comfort it had been—how it had eased the burden of intolerable strangeness which this universe imposes on us by dividing it into two halves and encouraging the mind never to think of both in the same context. What price we may have paid for this comfort in the way of false security and accepted confusion of thought is another matter.[4]

Chesterton enables us to see the natural and supernatural in light of each other and thus to see the world as it truly is. We have been conditioned to associate the mysterious and transcendent with fantasy or superstition in contrast to the real world of tangible facts. But tangible facts are only ever real (in the sense of being important) because of the intangible, mysterious reality of which they are a part.

The "spiritual sight" or general way of seeing the world for an ordinary, clear-headed person is "stereoscopic, like his physical sight: he sees two different pictures at once and yet sees all the better for that . . . The whole secret of mysticism is this: that

---

mind and matter.

4. Lewis, *Perelandra*, 11

man can understand everything by the help of what he does not understand."[5]

As is the case with the sun, "The one created thing which we cannot look at is the one thing in the light of which we look at everything."[6] He makes the distinction between "detached intellectualism"[7] and mysticism because it is specifically the detachment of the intellect from a power and knowledge that transcends it which hinders its function in accessing truth.

HIGH-STAKES PHILOSOPHICAL QUESTION

As is often the case in philosophy, questions that at first seem abstract and academic have profound implications for our everyday lives. As Chesterton explains,

> There are some people—and I am one of them—who think that the most practical and important thing about a man is still his view of the universe. We think that for a landlady considering a lodger, it is important to know his income, but still more important to know his philosophy. ... We think the question is not whether the theory of the cosmos affects matters, but whether in the long run, anything else affects them.[8]

Regarding the understanding of material objects as aspects or mediums of a greater reality, he saw that the denial of this results in an ephemeral, superficial view of human existence neutered of the spiritual life at the heart of any meaningful experience. A transcendent matrix of meaning may sound like the kind of thing semi-autistic philosophers debate about in the isolation of their faculty lounges, but the denial of this has as consequential an impact as a man's denial of his wife's faithfulness. A man who believes that his wife really does love him and one who believes his wife

5. Chesterton, *Orthodoxy*, 33
6. ibid
7. ibid
8. Chesterton, *Heretics*, 5

married only for money may both live in the same neighborhood and work for the same employer. The practical details of their daily lives may be almost identical, but what a difference there is in the actual living of that life! Our conception of the world determines the way we experience it. The pardoned prisoner and the death row inmate walk very differently down the same prison corridor.

Chesterton saw this danger in the popular "art for art's sake" movement propagated by prominent contemporary artists of his day, such as James Whistler and Walter Pater. To think of art as having a self-contained value independent of anything beyond itself instead of art as an intimation or a harbinger of a greater reality necessarily results in the shrinking of mental horizons. In that case, art cannot stir the heart *toward* anything. It cannot edify in the sense of building up, improving, or aligning one's character with the Good, the Beautiful, and the True. If there is no greater reality to which art makes us more attuned then there is only the pleasure of the immediate visual or audible sensation. In this view, art nourishes the soul as chewing gum nourishes the body. Chesterton proposes a contrast to put the point in perspective:

> We talk of some Whistlerian satire as a squib [firework]; but squibs can only shine in the dark. It is all the difference between the colors of fireworks that have their back to the vault of night and the colors of church windows that have their backs to the sun. For these people all the light of life was in the foreground; there was nothing in the background but an abyss.[9]

Few metaphors could be more revealing of the consequential difference between the two frameworks for understanding what matters in life. As explained in the passage from Bertrand Russell cited in Chapter Two, the purely material world "which science presents for our belief" is one in which the human mind compelled by fascination and the thirst for truth, and the human heart aching with desire for love and beauty, are just fireworks—ephemeral flashes that dissolve into darkness.

---

9. Chesterton, *Robert Louis Stevenson*, Chapter 4.

The difference between the worldviews represented by the squib and the stained glass is something like the difference between the maggot-filled eye sockets of a month-old corpse and the sparkling joy in the eyes of a year-old toddler. If the comparison seems exaggerated, consider again Bertrand Russell's conclusion about the highest of human experiences, "that no fire, no heroism, no intensity of thought and feeling, can preserve an individual life beyond the grave; that all the labors of the ages, all the devotion, all the inspiration, all the noonday brightness of human genius, are destined to extinction in the vast death of the solar system."[10] – or the proposition of the renowned neuroscientist and materialist V.S. Ramachandran that,

> All the richness of our mental life – all our feelings, our emotions, our thoughts, our ambitions, our love lives, our religious sentiments and even what each of us regards as his or her own intimate private self – is simply the activity of these little specks of jelly in our heads, in our brains. There is nothing else.[11]

When these propositions are taken seriously, it becomes clear that intellectually honest naturalists wouldn't have much to offer as motivational speakers. An honest college commencement speech given from the perspective of the squib mind might be something like the following:

"You should take great pride in the fact that the education you've received from this institution has enabled you to rise above the naivete of believing in fables about the kingdom come and life everlasting. Here and now is all there is, and now is your time. You're well aware that the greatest contributions you have to make to the world will ultimately be obliterated in the super nova. Nonetheless, I challenge you to strive to maximize your impact for the good. Even though in the end there will be neither anyone to remember you nor anything to be remembered, I challenge you

---

10. Russell, "A Free Man's Worship," first published as "The Free Man's Worship," Dec. 1903

11. V.S. Ramachandran, *A Brief Tour of Human Consciousness: From Impostor Poodles to Purple Numbers.*

to work and live in such a way that you will be remembered as a person who made a difference in this world."

One of the glaring ironies of scientism is the notion that the practice of science alone results in a greater capacity to move forward, make progress, and generally work to make a vibrant, flourishing world. To the contrary, if taken seriously and consistently, it is a philosophy that shrinks intellectual and emotional horizons to the most mundane and superficial level. The whole trajectory of thought is one of diminution, reduction, and constriction of human life—from the mystical soul to a conglomeration of cells.

SCIENTISM AND THE SPIRITUAL IMPOVERISHMENT OF SEX

A clear and highly consequential example of the emaciation of the soul that results from a myopically scientific worldview is the diminution of sex. In light of the contrast between the squib and the stained glass, the common reference to "fireworks" in alluding to sexual experience is much to the point. In the zeitgeist of the twenty-first century West, many people have done to sex what a toothless meth addict would do to the heirloom jewelry in his grandmother's safe. In the mind of the addict, the contents of the safe are just metal and rocks. Addiction shrinks and distorts his mental horizons blinding him to the value of anything beyond the next buzz. "All the light of life [is] in the foreground."

The sublime value of his grandmother's fifty-year-old wedding ring or his grandfather's purple heart has not changed. It is the addict's ability to see the real essence of these things that has changed. His bodily urges blind the eyes of his heart and mind so that the value of precious heirlooms can't compare to the hour of mindless ecstasy that comes from one hit. In something like a perverse reversal of the Midas touch, the squib mind turns transcendent wine into visceral water. Everything King Midas touched turned to gold, but every golden thing that can't be seen through a scientific lens turns to dross in the mind of the perceiver.

A comprehensive scientific explanation of two pigs copulating in a barnyard, for example, would entail an explanation of the way the neural signals in the brain of the male pig are triggered upon contact with the female resulting in agitation of certain glands which release reproductive hormones causing physiological changes in the male pig's sex organs which enable the transfer of sperm from the male into the uterus of the female. Those are the scientifically verifiable facts, and a scientific explanation of what goes on between a man and a woman in a honeymoon suite would be almost identical.

However, for a couple who are fully alive and in possession of all the faculties that distinguish them from pigs, there is a knowledge of something that occurs in the honeymoon suite that is to the copulation of pigs what a cathedral is to a cardboard box. The physical bodies and all the bio-chemical systems that comprise their sexual capacity are taken up into a transcendent, life-creating realm in which two souls are spiritually welded together so that neither are the same afterward.[12] The mind of scientism, in contrast, scoffs at the existence of such a transcendent realm because it can't be understood through a scientific assessment of reproductive organs. The one who only believes in science is prone to dismiss the spiritual significance of sex as lofty but scientifically ignorant traditionalism—to believe that there is no other realm for anything to be "taken up" into, and therefore there ultimately isn't much difference between the newlywed couple and the pigs in the barnyard.

There are also likely many people who would roll their eyes at the claim that sex is a sacred welding of souls because such a notion is so inconsistent with their experience. "I've slept with plenty of people," they might say. "There was nothing sacred about it. We were just using each other for a thrill." This perspective puts one in a similar state as the addict who sees nothing sacred in his grandmother's heirlooms. He just uses them for a thrill.

---

12. The noble force appointed to guard this sacred realm is called chastity.

THE ANTI-SCIENCE OF SCIENTISM

One of the greatest ironies of scientism is that it undermines the ability to think scientifically. The scientific method demands that we set aside personal biases and the nebulous assumptions of our cultural atmosphere and simply observe the phenomena that presents itself to our senses. Though the ethos of the method is to honestly observe and account for all the aspects of what it studies, many fundamental aspects of human experience and knowledge are not accounted for. What we see in observing human beings are creatures who are part of the natural world and yet repulsed by many aspects of that world—who have a keen sense of how the world *should* be in contrast to how it is—creatures who, in the midst of an imperfect and temporary world, are driven by a deep desire for permanence and for perfect[13] justice, beauty, love, and happiness—creatures who have an instinct for practical efficiency and survival, but are passionately motivated by impractical things like friendship, sports, and art which have no survival value.

One plausible hypothesis is that there is another realm, imperceptible to the five senses but utterly real, from which these seemingly alien desires originate and in which they will find their consummation. The concept of an Uncreated Creator who transcends time, space, and matter whose essence is reflected in our conscience and aesthetic sense—an Intelligent Mind from which intelligent creatures originate—makes for a metaphysical framework that fits our daily experiences and deepest desires like the glass slipper on the foot of Cinderella. The hypothesis proposed by the philosophy of naturalism, on the other hand, is summed up in the quote cited above from V.S. Ramachandran, that our thoughts, loves, religious convictions, and even our self-consciousness are "simply the activity of these little specks of jelly in our heads, in our brains. There is nothing else."[14]

---

13. In contrast to the innately temporary essence of the natural world, the concept of a perfect world necessarily implies eternity. Temporary love, beauty, and justice, by definition, are imperfect; permanence is an aspect of perfection.

14. V.S. Ramachandran, *A Brief Tour of Human Consciousness: From Impostor Poodles to Purple Numbers.*

Some philosophers who find this summation less than satisfying have suggested a theory of emergence to explain the reality of consciousness and conscience. There are different versions, but the basic idea is that the conscious, morally sensitive, human mind "emerges" at a point in the development of the brain when the level of physiological sophistication crosses a threshold resulting in the transition from unconscious matter to a conscious, personal being. This allows one to believe that matter, rather than spirit, is the fundamental reality, but that the conscious mind becomes distinct from matter once that threshold of development is crossed.

One analogy to illustrate this is something like a junior high science project demonstrating electrical current where a battery pack is attached to a piece of plywood. A wire connects the battery pack to a switch and the switch to a small fan motor. When the switch is flipped the fan rotates and the student proudly explains that the switch has channeled and directed the current from the battery pack to the fan. Now imagine the system becoming more complex by placing a paper windmill in front of the fan with its hub connected to a popsicle stick that moves when the fan is blown. The popsicle stick then taps a ping pong ball which then rolls down a chute and into a cup.

The question the emergent theory of consciousness raises is this: Is it reasonable to believe that the interactive points of the system could be multiplied in number and degrees of complexity to the point where the science experiment becomes conscious of itself? Could it be the case that when the eight-hundred-millionth device is wired into the chain, the whole system becomes aware of itself, and even impressed with itself, and able to decide whether it wants to continue expanding or instead feels a moral obligation to be content with the level of sophistication it already has as a good, virtuous science experiment should?

Among the main difficulties of this theory of consciousness is its ability to explain conscience. Whether or not the human mind emerged from an unconscious system of biological components into a conscious, morally sensitive state, if the mind is aware of ways a person should and should not behave, then such an awareness requires an authority—for which conscience is the mouthpiece—which, by definition, must be distinct from the mind that acknowledges it.

The theory of emergence may be thought of as an explanation of mind compatible with naturalist philosophy, but it can never be so. Since naturalism holds that there can be no spirit, mind, or will apart from matter, and that all that exists is the product of random, unintended motion, then no conscious mind could have emerged at all. An emerging mind first requires an increasingly complex system of tissues and neurochemistry, but "system" means a set of interacting parts set in a particular order to achieve an intended outcome. If there is no mind intending an order for the sake of a certain function, then there can be no such thing as a system of any kind. Contrary to common ways of talking, the notion of a "random system" is as self-contradictory as a square circle.

Because it is extremely hard to accept that an unbiased person could believe either a theory of purely material emergence, or Ramachandran's not-so-sunny proposition that our conscious life is the product of "specks of jelly" in our brains, the fact that many do claim to believe these is evidence of irrational bias and a particularly unscientific way of thinking. Bio-mechanical explanations of consciousness, meaning, and beauty make for good examples of science[15] sabotaged by scientism. It is nonsensical to suppose that a completely meaningless cosmos produced creatures who are psychologically dependent on the belief that life has meaning. Naturalist philosophy is scientifically inadequate because there is no place in it for the reality of the human mind. As Chesterton says about the response of Robert Louis Stevenson to pessimistic critics who thought that the poorly crafted characters and dingy materials of a toy theater were the only real facts of a children's play,

> He naturally answered: "My facts were my feelings; and what do you make of those facts? Either there is something in [toy theaters]; which you do not admit. Or else there is something in Life; which you also do not admit."

---

15. The basic concept of science (from the Latin "scientia") is the virtue of knowledge seeking.

> ... The realists, who overlook so many details, have never quite noticed where lay the falsity of their method; it lay in the fact that so long as it was materialistic, it could not really be realistic. For it could not be psychological. If toys and trifles can make people happy, that happiness is not a trifle and certainly cannot be a trick.[16]

A worldview cannot be realistic if it is not psychological because such a view takes no account of the psyche—the human self. This is why Chesterton criticizes the purely scientific thinker for "making himself inhuman in order to understand humanity."[17] It is a fact about fiction that fictional stories affect the hearts and minds of people at a deep level. It is a fact that toy theaters and simple tales evoke powerful feelings. This is a fact about human beings which naturalist thinkers simply don't account for. They are "realists who overlook so many details."

THE LIGHT FROM BEYOND THAT KEEPS SHINING THROUGH

When there is thought to be no light from beyond to illuminate the window of immediate experience it is exceedingly difficult to maintain a sense of purpose. It's hard to stay motivated to polish the brass on a sinking ship if one really does believe the ship is sinking. But inevitably materialist thinkers show that they don't really believe it. "Holding a philosophy which excludes humanity, they yet remain human."[18]

Russell, for example, continues from the point about the extinction of human achievement in the death of the solar system by concluding, "Only within the scaffolding of these truths, only on the firm foundation of unyielding despair, can the soul's habitation henceforth be safely built." Setting aside the contradiction (the soul's habitation cannot be "safely" built on despair; despair

---

16. Chesterton, *Robert Louis Stevenson*, Ch. 4
17. Chesterton, *Heretics*, 60
18. Lewis, *Miracles*, 52

is the thing from which the soul needs to be kept safe)—the mere fact that the soul needs a certain kind of "habitation" exposes the incoherence of his claim.

The (true) point Russell actually makes is contrary to the one he tries to argue. The irony is revealed in the word "habitation." An animal's natural habitat is not just a place where it is able to exist. The habitat is natural because the essence of the habitat correlates to the essence of the creature. Water is the natural habitat for fish because everything about the a fish—fins, gills, scales—corresponds with water and vice versa. It's not hard to imagine an arrangement where a fish could exist out of water, on a lab table with water pumped through tubes inserted into its gills, but this would not be the fish's "natural" habitat. The lab environment would allow the fish to exist but in a way that is contrary to its true essence as a fish.

To say, "Only on the scaffolding of these truths . . . can the soul's habitation be safely built," is to say that truth is the natural habitat for the human soul. It is to say that we are in the state that best correlates with our essence as human beings when our understanding is consistent with what is real. Along with love and beauty, truth is to human beings what water is to fish. In light of the purely physical world Russell claims to believe in, there is a contradiction in the notion that the soul is kept "safe" only by abiding in the truth.

We need to be kept safe from illusions and superstitions by aligning our beliefs with the truth because the truth is better. But it should be obvious that nothing can be better or worse in a world produced by an accidental collocation of atoms. Such a world simply exists as it exists. The mere suggestion of an ideal that tells us we have an obligation to align our beliefs with what is true is another way of saying that the world that exists should be conformed to something beyond it. No matter how adamantly atheists like Russell try to deny it, the transcendent light from beyond the window of the material world keeps shining through. As Peter Berger explains, "We are, then, faced with a quite simple alternative: Either we deny that there is here anything that can be called truth—a choice that would make us deny what we experience most profoundly as our own being; or we must look beyond the realm of our 'natural' experience for a validation of our certainty." Despite their philosophy, naturalists are constantly looking beyond the natural world for that validation.[19]

As with many believers in scientism, Russell is like the pessimistic philosopher, Dr. Emerson Eames, in Chesterton's *Manalive*. Eames explains to his particularly perceptive student, Innocent Smith, that there cannot be a merciful God because if there were,

> "[He[would put us out of our pain. He would strike us dead."
>
> "Why doesn't he strike us dead?" asked the undergraduate abstractedly, plunging his hands into his pockets.
>
> "He is dead himself," said the philosopher; "That is where he is really enviable."
>
> "To anyone who thinks, [he sees that] the pleasures of life, [are] trivial and soon tasteless, and bribes to bring us into a torture chamber. We all see that for any thinking man mere extinction is the . . ."

Eames is suddenly interrupted as his sympathetic student points a revolver at him and explains, "I'll help you out of your hole . . . It's not a thing I'd do for everyone, but you and I seem to have got so intimate tonight somehow. I know all your troubles now, and the only cure . . ."[20] Dr. Eames claims to believe that life is so pointless that extinction is its only remedy. Like Bertrand Russell, he suggests that the unyielding despair that comes from realizing the meaninglessness of life must be the foundation for the worldview of any intellectually respectable person. And yet, when he is faced with the imminent possibility of the extinction he claims to seek, a spark of desire for life suddenly appears on his dismal mental horizon. Contrary to the ostensible pessimism, Dr. Eames evades his student's offer to put him out of his misery by demanding that he put the gun away and rushes out of the window on to a ledge:

19. Berger, *A Rumour of Angels* 75
20. Chesterton, *Manalive*, 67.

"Let me come off this place," he cried. I can't bear it . . ."

" . . . I want the metaphysical point cleared up. Do I understand that you want to get back to life?"

"I'd give anything to get back," replied the unhappy professor.

The child-like Smith then gives a keen summary of the professor's duplicity which applies to many believers in scientism:

> I'll just tell you this to wind up with. If you really were what you profess to be, I don't see that it would matter to snail or seraph if you broke your impious stiff neck and dashed out all your driveling devil-worshipping brains. But in strict biographical fact you are a very nice fellow, addicted to talking putrid nonsense, and I love you like a brother.[21]

Like Chesterton himself, Innocent Smith sees life through theories about life. As with Dr. Eames, Bertrand Russell and so many others develop a dark, distorted, and inhumane perspective on life by forming beliefs from the calculating intellect detached from the rest of the person. Theirs is the philosophy of the severed head. But inevitably, despite doctrinaire, pessimistic conclusions, when life is truly threatened, the whole person is suddenly reengaged, and it is only the whole person fully alive who can set the head in its rightful place.

The Bertrand Russells of the world conceive of themselves as sober-minded adults who, in contrast to sentimental and religiously blinded children, see the world as it truly is and proceed to build a "firm foundation of unyielding despair" for the habitation of the soul. And yet they do so while believing they are engaged in the noble, courageous, honorable endeavor of truth-seeking. In other words, their motivation for denying that there is any light beyond the window of the world is a sense of virtue that is wholly dependent on that light.

---

21. ibid

CHAPTER 7

Gratitude and the Grammar of God

"I had always vaguely felt facts to be miracles in the sense that they are wonderful: now I began to think them miracles in the stricter sense that they were *willful*."

G.K. Chesterton, *Orthodoxy*

READING CHESTERTON IS AN experience of inchoate clarity like waking from rapidly diminishing anesthesia because of his tendency to see the real essence of something rather than theories about it. He presents obvious and immediate things in such a way as to show that the tendency to perceive the familiar as uninteresting is typically the result of blindness caused by repetition, because "grown-up people are not strong enough to exult in monotony."[1] There are few better examples of his ability to bring the reality of commonplace things into a dazzling light than his explanation of one of the most constant of commonplace events as explained in a critique of H.G. Wells' *The Time Machine*:

> In that sublime nightmare the hero saw trees shoot up like green rockets, and vegetation spread visibly like a green conflagration, or the sun shoot across the sky from east to west with the swiftness of a meteor. Yet in his sense these things were quite as natural when they went

1. Chesterton, *Orthodoxy*, 65

swiftly; and in our sense they are quite as supernatural when they go slowly. The ultimate question is why they go at all; and anybody who really understands that question will know that it always has been and always will be a religious question; or at any rate a philosophical or metaphysical question.[2]

What could be more easily taken for granted than the sun in the sky? A work of science fiction that imagines it shooting from one horizon to the other in one hour instead of twelve sparks a wild fascination that causes us to perceive it as magical. But lengthening the duration of its movement in no way diminishes the magic. This, indeed, raises an acutely metaphysical question. The age-old philosophical question is why there is something rather than nothing, but an earth revolving around a blazing, illuminate ball which provides the warmth and light on which the entire planet depends is more than just "something." Why a single day consists of such a life-giving cosmic spectacle is a thoroughly fascinating question, but even more so is the question of why the planet is filled with people so intrigued by that spectacle that they would make poems and paintings about it and develop whole scientific fields of study to better understand it.

At a more fundamental level than our artistic and intellectual interest, the fact that we are here at all is a stunning reality: "The sense of the miracle of humanity itself should be always more vivid to us than any marvels of power, intellect, art, or civilization. The mere man on two legs, as such, should be felt as something more heartbreaking than any music and more startling than any caricature."[3] This is the Chesterton effect, to open our eyes to the essence of immediate realities to which we've become blind through familiarity and the zeitgeist.

Another familiar but rarely examined experience which he brings to light is one of the most consistent themes in his work and most distinct characteristics of his outlook and personality. Ironically, it is a topic on which he is widely quoted by those who

2. Chesterton, *The Everlasting Man*, 25
3. ibid

do not share his Christian beliefs and a point which is as strong an evidence for the existence of the Christian God as anything else he writes about. In his autobiography, he explains the perspective he held in his young life before embracing any well-developed religious doctrine:

> At the back of our brains, so to speak, there was a forgotten blaze or burst of astonishment at our own existence. The object of the artistic and spiritual life was to dig for this submerged sunrise of wonder; so that a man sitting in a chair might suddenly understand that he was actually alive, and be happy.[4]

In a later chapter, he recollects his boyhood reflection on the wonder in perceiving the beauty of the simplest things in the natural world. "I asked through what incarnations or prenatal purgatories I must have passed to earn the reward of looking at a dandelion."[5]

He says that taking things with gratitude instead of taking them for granted is "the chief idea of my life."[6] In describing the thought process by which he developed his own personal heresy which, much to his surprise, turned out to be the fundamentals of Christian orthodoxy, he explains that,

> The test of all happiness is gratitude; and I felt grateful, though I hardly knew to whom. Children are grateful when Santa Claus puts in their stockings gifts of toys or sweets. Could I not be grateful to Santa Claus when he put in my stockings the gift of two miraculous legs? We thank people for birthday presents of cigars and slippers. Can I thank no one for the birthday present of birth?[7]

With a child-like purity of vision, Chesterton uncovers acute beauties long buried under deadening scientific reductionism, social pretension, and the numb-hearted, doctrinaire affectation too common among well-educated people. Like Innocent Smith,

---

4. Chesterton, *The Autobiography of G.K. Chesterton*, 60
5. Chesterton, *The Autobiography of G.K. Chesterton*, 223
6. ibid
7. Chesterton, *Orthodoxy*, 60

the protagonist of his *Manalive*, he "had somehow made the giant stride from babyhood to manhood and missed that crisis in youth when most of us grow old."[8] Gratitude is the clarifying lens which enables him to see the intrinsic beauty in the world without the dullness and distortion of vision that inevitably results from taking things for granted.

To some, this may seem like an uplifting but ultimately platitudinous point. The fact that atheists are in a conundrum when they feel thankful but have no one to thank, or that we should be more grateful for the two feet that fill our stockings than we are for the candy that fills them at Christmas—these may seem like only tongue-and-cheek quips characteristic of the jovial Chesterton who liked to season his prose with provocative one-liners. But with his emphasis on gratitude he brings into focus a phenomenon which can affect the unsuspecting secular mind like a door knob turning from the inside in an erstwhile empty house.

THE THANK IN NEED OF A YOU

The force of the point can only be felt when one thinks thoroughly and deeply about what gratitude is, what it's like to experience it, and how fundamental it is to human psychology. Gratitude is a response, and the nature of a response is distinctly different from other experiences. I can feel exhilaration, for example, standing in the surf when my feet lose contact with the sandy ground as my body is lifted by a wave and forced toward the shore, but exhilaration is not a response. It is an effect. It is an inner experience which is intransitive in nature.

In English grammar the difference between transitive and intransitive verbs is in the description of action on its own and an action transferred from one thing to another. An intransitive verb acts on its own, as with the word "rises" in "The sun rises." But a transitive verb extends an action from a subject to a receiving object, as with "raises" in "He raises the flag." If I'm lifted by a

---

8. Chesterton, *Manalive*, 14.

swelling ocean wave at the beach, then the wave is the cause, and the exhilaration is the effect, but once that effect occurs in me it does not extend beyond me. The exhilaration itself is not an action that transfers from me, the subject, to a receiving object. The experience need not extend beyond my own consciousness, but this is not the case with gratitude which is inherently transitive. The essence of gratitude is a trajectory from receiver to giver. A person cannot be grateful *for* something without owing gratitude *to* someone. This is just the nature of the experience.

One uniquely helpful means of illuminating the real essence of what certain words describe is sign language. Words with their elastic connotations can mislead or obscure the reality of the things they point to, but when signs and movements are used the movements often illustrate the true nature of the thing. There are few better examples of this than the gesture for "thank you"—an open hand thrust outward from the chin. Exactly!—an inward to outward trajectory—from me, the one who is thankful, to you, the one I thank. The gesture physically demonstrates the essence of what's being described.

Along with the necessarily transitive nature of gratitude, another essential aspect of the experience is that it is a *response* to an act of personal will.[9] Thankfulness is intrinsically personal. It is unintelligible apart from the intentional, uncoerced act of a giver. Upon receiving a gift, the words "thank you" are instinctively followed by "you didn't have to do that," because the first phrase is logically dependent on the second. We thank the gift-giver specifically because she "didn't have to" give. "Thank you. You didn't have to do that" is an abbreviated way of saying, "I am grateful to you because you expressed concern for me by intentionally prioritizing my well-being. You could have directed your attention, resources, and efforts elsewhere, but you valued me more than other things. I am grateful because I know that the gift I have received was not

---

9. "Personal will," like the term "free will," is a tautology, like referring to a three-sided triangle or a fish that swims. For an action to be willed or intended necessarily means it was intended by a person. If an act of the will does not originate in a person, then it is not a "free" act of the will.

inevitable. I only received it because you chose to give it to me when you could have chosen differently."

This is not just one way of thinking about gratitude. It is the essence of what gratitude is. One cannot experience it in the absence of an intentional, freely chosen act. For example, if a student named John presents me with a gift at the end of a semester and says, "I want to give you this as a token of my appreciation for you as a teacher," this would be meaningful to me, and I would respond by saying "Thank you, John. You didn't have to do that." If, after John leaves the room, someone from the computer science department comes to me and asks about my experience of having John as a student, I would say something like, "John has been a great student, and he was very generous in giving me a gift."

But if the computer science person then tells me that John's full name is John:T3ss2b, and that he is actually not a human but a highly sophisticated android prototype programmed to act as a student and give gifts to all his teachers—upon hearing this, any gratitude I would feel from receiving John's gift would instantly vanish. I would only have thanked him for the gift because he freely chose to give it, because he "didn't have to do that." But if he did have to do it because he had been programmed to do so, then there would be no intentional act to be thankful for and no person to thank, or if there was a person to thank it would not be John. In that case, thanking John would not only be inappropriate but unintelligible. The only reasonable thing to do would be to find the computer scientist who programmed John and thank him for the gift since he would be the one who *meant* to give it. Gratitude only makes sense if it is a response to the person who intended the thing for which one is grateful. In light of this, when one considers the pervasive and instinctual phenomenon of gratitude in response to "gifts" like good health and the beauty of the natural world when there is no immediately identifiable giver, then a certain reality begins to appear on the outskirts of one's mental horizons—a Transcendent Giver.

SOMETHING HAS BEEN DONE

That Giver is alluded to in Chesterton's explanation of the difference in conceptions of the natural world held by irreligious scientists and what he calls "fairy-tale philosophers." Regarding the scientists, he explains:

> I found the whole modern world talking scientific fatalism; saying that everything is as it must always have been, being unfolded without fault from the beginning. The leaf on the tree is green because it could never have been anything else.[10]

In dramatic contrast, the fairy-tale philosopher,

> is glad that the leaf is green precisely because it might have been scarlet. He feels as if it had turned green an instant before he looked at it. He is pleased that snow is white on the strictly reasonable ground that it might have been black. Every color has in it a bold quality as of choice; the red of garden roses is not only decisive but dramatic, like suddenly spilt blood. He feels that something has been *done*.[11]

Inherent in the response of gratitude is an awareness of contingency. Just as the meaning of an unexpected gift from a friend is in the fact that he "didn't have to do that," the gratitude evoked by stunning natural beauty comes from a clear sense that it didn't have to be like that. A snow-capped mountain ridge glowing in dawn light or a crimson cardinal perched on a white dogwood blossom could have been otherwise, but we are thankful that they are what they are.

The luxurious oscillation of waves dissolving on a beach interspersed with the echo of gulls overhead, the smell of coffee, the taste of strawberries, the sound of an ecstatic infant's giggle—such experiences stir a distinct sensation in people which is appropriately expressed with the words "thank you." In other words, the

---

10. Chesterton, *Orthodoxy*, 64
11. ibid

nature of that deep sense which we call gratitude, so naturally evoked by these kinds of experiences, is the distinct sense that we've been given a gift that didn't have to be given. We extol, praise, sing, and thank in response to something that is but didn't have to be. Of course, not all people feel a sense of gratitude in response to experiences like these, but those who don't are the exception to the rule. Moreover, an absence of gratitude usually aligns with an absence of humility, charity, and open-mindedness, so that those who don't see any reasons to be grateful typically don't see many other things that are also crucial to human flourishing.

THE GRAMMAR OF GOD

Grammar is defined as a system and structure of language. It is something like a rule book which enables us to make sense of how we communicate, and it is a rule book that is both prescriptive and descriptive. Like the rule book for a sport, it is prescriptive in giving the rules by which the game must be played, but descriptive in that the rules simply describe the nature of the game. The basic rules of baseball, for example, require that the game is played on a diamond shaped field, and that the defensive team must always have possession of the ball. These rules prescribe the basics of how baseball should be played, but they also simply describe what baseball is. If the players aren't playing by these rules they're not playing baseball.

As with rules for a game, there are grammatical rules prescribed for the right way to communicate. But those rules are actually just a description of how communication works. If I were to say, "All the boy Finnish they're exam with thyme left," then I would be breaking the grammatical rules of communication, and in doing so I would no longer be communicating since it would be impossible to know what I was intending to say. Grammar is the way language is structured so that it can do what language is supposed to do.

Likewise, gratitude is the way the human mind is structured so that people can live the kind of lives they're supposed to live.

Gratitude is a fundamental rule in the rule book of humanity. It is prescriptive in that it makes us aware of the attitude we should have; we know we *should* be grateful for good things. It is also descriptive in that it simply describes one of the aspects of a whole and healthy human being. The fact that gratitude is one of the most significant factors in fortifying against depression shows that it is an essential aspect of true flourishing. That which is necessary for psychological health is, by definition, integral to human essence.[12]

Conversely, ingratitude and entitlement are universally recognized as character flaws. A void of gratitude is evidence of a corrupted or pathological mind. To live a fully human life is to live within a charged circuit of love that moves in perpetual reciprocity from people who are thankful for what they've been given to the Giver without whom the thanks is nonsensical. Gratitude is a trajectory of the human heart that terminates in the heart of God. It is the grammar of human flourishing because it is the grammar of God.

It is also sobering to realize that the guilt conscientious people feel when they realize they've not been grateful, or charitable, or honest also points to the same Divine Person. Like gratitude, guilt is unintelligible unless it is personal. When one honestly reflects on the nature of the experience, it is clear that guilt is an awareness of personal betrayal. Gratitude is the knowledge that we owe thanks to a person who intended something for our good; guilt is the knowledge that we have betrayed a person to whom we should be loyal. One may feel frustrated, angry, or stupid when caught violating parking laws or regulations for building permits, but that is a very different thing from guilt. The feeling of guilt is more like the emotion a person feels upon seeing the disappointment on a friend's face the moment he learns that he's been lied to.

As with the impulse to give thanks for things that no human could give us, the experience of feeling guilty for something which

12. "Psyche" means "self." Psychology is the study of the self, and psychological health means a human person maintaining a mindset and habitual behaviors that are consistent with an ideal human nature—just as a dog that barks and chases balls and a bird that flies and lays eggs are creatures living rightly as they function according to their natures.

no other person knows about points to the Person who does know. Conscience works like the name of a man's wife tattooed on his arm which he must read as he waves at the prostitute who tempts him. Conscience is the heart of God tattooed on the mind of man, and guilt is the awareness that we have betrayed the one to whom we're supposed to be faithful.

THANKFUL BUT THOUGHTLESS

The religiously skeptical reader may be indignant at this point. To say that such a basic, universal, and seemingly ambiguous human experience like gratitude is clear evidence of the existence of God will sound to some like ham-fisted proselytizing in the absence of a sound argument. Such was the response Chesterton anticipated:

> For the first thing the casual critic will say is "What nonsense all this is; do you mean that a poet cannot be thankful for grass and wild flowers without connecting it with theology; let alone your theology?" To which I answer, "Yes; I mean he cannot do it without connecting it with theology, unless he can do it without connecting it with thought. If he can manage to be thankful when there is nobody to be thankful to, and no good intentions to be thankful for, then he is simply taking refuge in being thoughtless in order to avoid being thankless."[13]

The last line is key. The irony is that antireligious bias prevents one from thinking about the nature and implications of gratitude, but there is an inherent moral obligation in the experience of gratitude which makes it painfully clear that we *should* be grateful. The impulse of gratitude is so strong that one who refuses to believe there is someone to thank will still be thankful, like a person who doesn't believe in the existence of birds but is compelled to fill the bird feeder with seeds every morning nonetheless.

This is the point of the quip Chesterton cites from the English artist Rossetti that, "The worst moment for the atheist is when he

---

13. Chesterton, *The Autobiography of G.K. Chesterton*, 227

is really thankful and has nobody to thank."[14] It is the worst moment because of the self-inflicted incongruity, not like a hungry man who can't find food, but a hungry man who has been taught to believe that food is an empty myth invented by ignorant people in the past. Not only would his body remain hungry, but his mind would remain confused as he is forced to experience hunger as a desire *for* something while believing it to be a desire for nothing.

Like gratitude, the essence of hunger is a desire in search of fulfillment. Both gratitude and hunger have an imperative essence—a nonnegotiable *must* that compels a person to seek the object of desire. (Consider how frustrating it is to be thankful for a gift when there is no way of contacting the person who gave it). Gratitude places a burden on the soul to thank in a similar way hunger places a burden on the body to eat. But if one believes the thing to which the desire is oriented doesn't exist, then he must live in the hopeless dissonance, not of unfulfilled but of unfulfillable desire. This requires a person to defy reason and the plain dictates of observation by redefining the experience as something other than a desire *for something*.

AN ALIEN INTERVIEW

Since familiarity dulls the senses and those who see things most clearly are often those seeing them for the first time, it may be helpful to imagine an interstellar alien explorer from a faraway galaxy who travels to earth on a data-gathering mission to learn about human thought and behavior. For the sake of the analogy we'll assume the alien has learned English but has had no exposure to American politics, North Korea, Vladimir Putin, Nietzsche, reality TV, K-pop, injury attorneys, or sauerkraut, as a knowledge of these would inevitably compel the alien to assign earth to an intergalactic list of prohibited planets and avoid entering our solar system at all costs.

---

14. Chesterton, *St. Francis of Assisi*, 58

Gratitude and the Grammar of God

We'll imagine the alien landing on a public university campus somewhere in the United States. After a thorough interview with a psychology professor about the nature of the human experience of gratitude—what it is and how it plays into people's psychological wellbeing—he then meets with a professor of evolutionary psychology to get further insight on the newly discovered phenomenon.

Alien: I've just learned about the basic human experience you call gratitude. You are a professor not only of the human self but of the process by which humans and everything else on your planet developed over time. How do you understand gratitude in light of evolutionary development?

Professor: The propensity for gratitude in human beings inevitably evolved over many billions of years to provide a survival advantage by securing the protection of stronger and more resourceful benefactors who can shield a person from predators and other threats. The more one thanks someone stronger or wealthier than himself, the more likely the stronger person is to develop an affinity for the one expressing gratitude and thus protect him from danger.

Alien: Your explanation appears to be incongruent with the essence of that which it seeks to explain. Humans universally describe the experience of gratitude as a response to a gift, not a means of self-preservation. A gift, by definition, is uncoerced and motivated by a genuine concern for the well-being of the receiver. If that which evokes the response of gratitude is not a freely given gift then there would be nothing for a human to be grateful for.

Professor: Well, that is the way we tend to think of it, but in reality gratitude is only a survival mechanism.

Alien: So, what humans perceive as a response to an uncoerced gift— either from other humans or a transcendent, personal Giver—you believe to be an illusion? You conclude that what they experience as a dynamic reciprocity of love and gratitude is actually nothing more than a mechanical, cost-benefit calculation in pursuit of survival advantage?

Professor: That is correct.

Alien: In researching your planet prior to my arrival, I read the works of a human philosopher named William of Ockham. He is well known among your kind for a principle called "Ockham's razor" which says that the simplest explanation is most likely the accurate one.

Since gratitude is experienced as a response to an intentional, personal act of benevolence, wouldn't it be more reasonable to conclude that such acts do occur, and in cases where one feels grateful for something no human could be responsible for, wouldn't it be more reasonable to conclude that the desire to give thanks suggests there is a Divine Giver to whom thanks should be given?

Professor: That's impossible.

Alien: How do you know?

Professor: Because Charles Darwin said so.

Alien: While waiting in your office before you arrived, I noticed you have displayed on your bookshelf a card with words written in a barely readable script, apparently from a small human you helped produce, which reads, "Thank you for being such a great Daddy."

I also noticed a framed letter from one of your students thanking you for your excellence as a teacher and the concern you have for students' success. Why would you have any interest in publicly displaying the self-interested attempts of other humans to secure a survival advantage?

Gratitude and the Grammar of God

Professor: Well, those are quite a different matter.

Alien: {After making a few notes on his digital wristband}
I have concluded you are a bad scientist because your conclusions do not comport with the facts you observe. I plan to broadcast a message through your nation's electronic media platforms warning that you and your kind should not be allowed to leave the university. If your way of thinking ever influences those who make laws and collect taxes, your civilization may be in danger of collapsing.

CHAPTER 8

That Which is Stronger Than Sorrow or Joy

> Mountain sunsets
> And starry-cold skies
> Are a bath for the soul,
> Making my heart hearken
> To obvious secrets
> Yet untold.

IN TOLSTOY'S NOVELLA, *The Death of Ivan Ilyich*, Ivan lives a highly successful and completely pathetic life. Though professionally and financially accomplished, he is an utterly superficial man whose horizons of thought never extend beyond a concern for upwardly mobile social connections and carefully chosen home furnishings that reflect an upper class status. At the height of his deceptive success, Ivan contracts a terminal illness and is forced to spend long hours ruminating on the emptiness of his marriage and the absence of any genuine passion for the achievements of his life, as all his choices have been oriented around a meaningless social hierarchy. His unwelcomed reflections then culminate in a dark epiphany. It was, "as if I was going steadily downhill, while imagining I was going up. And so it was. In public opinion I was going uphill, and exactly to that extent life was slipping away from under me ... And now that's it, so die!"[1]

The trajectory of Ivan's life also reflects the trajectory of a life lived by the lights of scientism. If it is true, "That Man is the product of causes which had no prevision of the end they were achieving; that his origin, his growth, his hopes and fears, his loves and his beliefs, are but the outcome of accidental collocations of atoms,"[2] then common secular notions of purpose—such as the perception of an increasingly just and rational world realized by the liberation of the intellect from the shackles of oppressive tradition—are imaginary, just like Ivan's perception of success. Secular scientists imagine themselves living victorious lives by moving out of the mire of a religious worldview and up the hill of intellectual discovery, while in reality the necessary implications of their philosophy make both victory and fulfillment impossible.

However, the parallel with Ivan is not exact. He has bitter regret upon realizing he had wasted much of his life and is thus unfulfilled at the end, but if one embraces the view of scientism so clearly and honestly articulated by Bertrand Russell, the very notion of wasting one's life or living a fulfilling life is gibberish. Likewise, the distinction between real and imaginary is nonsensical, as is the whole paradigm of naturalist philosophy. It cannot be reasonably described or even critiqued because it undermines language and thought.

We can say with certainty that if the world really is nothing more than the result of a cosmic accident, then any concept of success is a delusion. We could say that everything in the world is nothing more than a chaotic array of cosmic flotsam, but this turns out to be another inapplicable metaphor. Flotsam is the floating debris from a shipwreck, but "wreck" implies something that has gone off course, and if "man is the product of causes which had no prevision of the end they were achieving," then there was never an intended course to begin with.

---

1. Tolstoy, *The Death of Ivan Ilyich*, 120
2. Russell, "A Free Man's Worship," first published as "The Free Man's Worship," Dec. 1903

It is an immutable fact that an "accidental collocation of atoms" cannot produce meaning or fulfillment. It cannot produce truth or virtue, success or failure, wisdom or stupidity. It cannot produce the intellectual courage to follow the scientific facts wherever they may lead. It cannot produce inspiration, aspiration, motivation, or contemplation, nor can it produce judgment, will, or choice of any kind. The difference between a person's self-perception and the reality of his character, as with Ivan Ilyich, is no more or less significant than the difference between a shark's tooth and a racoon's intestine. In a word, a world that is purely the outcome of an accidental collision of blind, impersonal forces is a dead world. No matter how strong the sense of moving up the hill of discovery and enlightenment, an accidental, material world void of any immaterial will or mind can only lead downhill into moral anomie and intellectual abyss.

A DIMMING WORLD

Nietzsche's famous madman carries a lantern in the daytime of a nineteenth-century European city, proclaiming to the people that "God is dead." But he eventually realizes that he has come too soon. " 'I come too early,' he then said; 'my time is not yet.' This tremendous event is still on its way, wandering; it has not yet reached the ears of men."[3] The point is that the well-educated citizens claim to disbelieve but still behave as if God exists.

Though Nietzsche himself was a madman, his fictional madman speaks the truth in proclaiming that many people in the Western world in the past two centuries have claimed to be too scientifically enlightened to believe in God and yet have continued to live by the light of a Christian worldview. Unlike the more naïve atheists in the early twenty-first century, Nietzsche understood with unusual clarity that the concept of universal human rights, the virtue of mercy, and the moral obligation to care for the weakest

---

3. Nietzsche, *The Gay Science*, Section 125

among us are distinctly Christian values (all of which he thought pathetic, a "slave morality," which was ruinous for society).

But the engine of Western civilization can only run on the fumes of Christianity for so long. Our behaviors are always directed by a metaphysical framework, which is to say we behave according to what we believe the world is really like. From this symbiotic relationship between beliefs and behavior comes the moral sensibilities that define a culture. Over time, those sensibilities forge cultural habits which are not easily broken. Like the person who continues to flip the light switch upon entering a room after the power has been out for hours, the moral and behavioral habits of a culture will continue for a time even when a majority no longer believe in the Divine power that orients the behavior. But this won't last forever. It may take time, but the person in the dark house will eventually realize the lights are off and stop trying to turn them on. Likewise, a post-Christian society with a long history of incremental dimming will eventually come to believe the Light is out altogether and accommodate itself to darkness without the vestige of illuminating virtues.

In the 1960's many young people across the Western world realized they did not believe in the God who created sex for marriage and liberated their libidos from the oppression of self-discipline. Since then, many have realized that they do not believe in the God who makes us responsible for our sexual behavior and have liberated themselves from the burden of parenthood. More recently, some have realized they don't believe in the God who created humans male and female and have liberated themselves from their genitals.

Scientism, as it is diffused into the intellectual atmosphere of Western culture, is a catalyst of atrophy that will eventually lead people to liberate themselves even further. We are told that "the world which science presents for our belief" is a world in which spiritual beings are impossible, and, therefore, a world with no room for God. But if this is true then it is also a world with no room for people. If spiritual beings aren't possible, then people cannot be spiritual beings and cannot be *inspired* as they yearn for purpose, meaning, beauty, love, and justice, all of which are, in the science-only view, only unintentional artifacts of an accident. Upon this realization, many will liberate themselves from life altogether, though for a whole society, this doesn't happen with a sudden and dramatic act of suicide.

MUSCLING OUR WAY PAST THE GAG REFLEX

In the 2007 animated film, Ratatouille, Remy, the rat, has an exceptionally delicate palate and aspires to be a chef—a tough ambition given the lack of hospitality for rats in restaurant kitchens. He can't understand the dietary habits of other members of his rat family, but his brother gives some insight in response to Remy's disgust at the thought of eating garbage: "If you can muscle your way past the gag reflex, all kinds of food possibilities open up." The worldview of scientism makes it much easier to muscle our way past the gag reflex, because, in that view, the conscience and convictions that make us gag at immoral behavior are not spiritual in nature but *only* the product of biochemicals. If that's the case, then what makes a person gag at the thought of Nazi medical experiments is the same kind of thing that makes a person gag after eating undercooked chicken. Such an absurd comparison is hard to swallow, so to speak, and the process on a societal level can be a long and gradual one, but each gulp makes the next one easier. The difference with the expansion of food possibilities in Ratatouille is that the muscling past moral and rational gag reflexes does not lead to new possibilities but impossibilities. It is a transition from the higher to the lower—from nobility to noir, from the sublime to the soulless suburb, from the hope of heavenly glory to hoping that muffins are on sale at Costco.

Prescientific people once thought a man swallowing fear and sacrificing himself in defense of his family was the essence of valor. But we now know that valor, like all virtues, is "just" a psychological effect of social conditioning which functions to sustain the species. It was also once thought (by Jews and Christians, at least) that sex is a holy and powerful act which ratifies, through something like a welding of human souls, the spousal relationship which is the exclusive and mystical means of generating new human life. But we now know that the neuro-chemical process of arousal and copulation occurring in a honeymoon suite has little biological variance from that which occurs in the bodies of two pigs in a barnyard. And on it goes. All the awe and wonder—the rapture of love and beauty, the dread of evil and darkness—all come to be seen under laboratory lights as "just" bio-mechanical processes whose only value, despite the grand illusion of transcendence, is survival. Scientism is the catalyst which propels a society down a trajectory of banality which ends in the suffocation of the soul. A world where randomly evolved chemicals are thought to explain all that was once attributed to the spirits of people and the Spirit of God is, obviously, a spiritless world. Like a spiritless body, there is no life in it.

In the past, a person could see an array of electric color in a tulip bed swaying in a May breeze and be struck with the sense that it was an ember scattered from a fire of joy kindled in the heavens. A man could kiss a woman for the first time and feel as if he'd been knighted by a star. One could become suddenly weak-kneed in awe at the sight of the ocean from a cliff top and feel the urge to cover his mouth like Job, enamored with the crushing beauty that is a glimmer of the heart of God.

When these experiences are no longer understood as windows through which we see the transcendent life but only dopamine networks, neurons, and accidentally conditioned hormone surges with no purpose but enhancing chances for survival, the effect of such a shift in perspective is the opposite of enlightenment. Living in such a world (if one can consistently believe in such a world) is like living in a room with constricting walls, dimming lights, and depleting oxygen. It is a windowless room where one can no longer be inspired by other worldly things because there is no other world.

This lifeless room and the "unyielding despair" of those who must occupy it is the place which Bertrand Russell says must be the habitation of the soul according to the dictates of science. And this is the room which Chesterton smashes into like a wrecking ball, crumbling the morbid bricks of scientism and flooding the suffocating darkness with the fresh air and warm light of true life.

THE LIFE WITHIN AND THE EMPTINESS OF EFFICIENCY

In response to critics of Charles Dickens who said the characters in his novels were too exaggerated and unrealistic, Chesterton writes a paragraph that dissipates the soul-denying myopia of naturalist philosophy like blazing sunbeams on a frost-covered windowpane. Dickens' critics said his portrayals,

> were not "like life," and there, they thought, was an end of the matter, [but] men saw that it was necessary to give a much deeper and more delicate meaning to the expression "like life." Streets are not life, cities and civilisations are not life, faces even and voices are not life itself. Life is within, and no man hath seen it at any time. As for our meals, and our manners, and our daily dress, these are things exactly like sonnets; they are random symbols of the soul. One man tries to express himself in books, another in boots; both probably fail. Our solid houses and square meals are in the strict sense fiction. They are things made up to typify our thoughts. The coat a man wears may be wholly fictitious; the movement of his hands may be quite unlike life . . . For Dickens is "like life" in the truer sense, in the sense that he is akin to the living principle in us and in the universe; he is like life, at least in this detail, that he is alive.[4]

The same life that moves a scientist to prioritize the study of photosynthesis and cell multiplication also moves him to prefer working next to the window overlooking evergreens in the park and to wear a green sweater rather than a gray hoodie. The life that invigorates a man upon making a discovery about black holes is also the life that motivates him to wear a black tie to a dinner

---

4. Chesterton, *Charles Dickens*, 9

That Which is Stronger Than Sorrow or Joy

party. "When a man has discovered why men in Bond Street wear black hats he will at the same moment have discovered why men in Timbuctoo wear red feathers."[5]

The life that makes us alive in the most real sense of the word is, *zoe*.[6] It is what makes me, me and you, you. It is the life within that causes a person to be so deeply fascinated by astronomy and so deeply moved by a symphony. *Zoe* is the impassioned and impractical heart of a human being. It manifests in our carefully arranged "meals, and our manners, and our daily dress." It is expressed in our insistence on color and collars.[7] The *zoe* within is evident in every human expression from architecture to argyle socks. It is the life of love and loyalty, of play and frivolity, of honor and elegance. Dismissing or denying this kind of life because it cannot be scientifically quantified would be no less absurd and no less destructive than dismissing oxygen because it cannot be seen or eaten.

Denying the spiritual aspects of life results in a pathological reversal of ends and means where the personal and meaningful is sacrificed for the mechanical and practical. A truly flourishing, humane society is one where scientific discoveries, technological advancements, and economic systems must always be in service to the life of the soul. The prioritization of technology and practical efficiency over the spiritual life inevitably moves individuals and societies into a state of ennui where a rich intellectual and emotional life is anesthetized by a concern for pragmatic efficiency and perpetual pleasantness. As Chesterton explains,

> When everything about a people is for the time growing weak and ineffective, it begins to talk about efficiency. So it is that when a man's body is a wreck he begins, for the first time, to talk about health. Vigorous organisms talk not about their processes, but about their aims . . .

---

5. Chesterton, *Heretics*, 60

6. The ancient Greek word for spiritual life, in contrast to "bios," the physical processes or chronologies of life.

7. The fact that neckties and food coloring exist is proof of the spiritual nature of man.

> None of the strong men in the strong ages would have understood what you meant by working for efficiency.[8]

When the life within grows cold because we've been duped into believing that we're not actually humans but only an assortment of cells, then we no longer pursue the "high and wild ideals"[9] that make life worth living and focus instead on efficiency. We leave philosophical and religious concerns behind and develop more powerful technology to help us do nothing more efficiently.

This results in a world Ray Bradbury saw with eerie prescience when he wrote about a futuristic dystopia where people have traded truth for tranquility and, in the absence of a thought life, are in constant need of mindless visceral stimulation. When transcendent longings have faded with the spiritual anesthesia of scientism, all that's left to demand our attention are "clubs and parties . . . acrobats and magicians, dare-devils, jet cars, motorcycle helicopters, sex and heroin, more of everything to do with automatic reflex."[10] It is a world, not unlike ours, with full refrigerators and empty souls, bright phone screens and dark minds, where cathedrals are replaced with strip malls and love with dopamine.

Bradbury's dystopian *Fahrenheit 451* is not a critique of scientism, *per se*. It satirizes a society that prioritizes superficial tranquility at the expense of contemplation and truth-seeking, but the dystopian world he describes is also the eventual fate of a culture that equates belief in the supernatural with superstition.

ALIVE IN A DEAD WORLD

When God becomes unreal in the minds of people, they may still claim to believe, but claims and questions about God are no longer thought to be important enough to risk the tension or discomfort that can result from publicly proclaiming and debating such questions. Thus, religion is relegated to the private sphere, like an

---

8. Chesterton, *Heretics*, 6
9. ibid
10. Bradbury, *Fahrenheit 451*, 61

interest in coin collecting or Bigfoot sightings. But those who are truly alive are obsessed with questions of transcendent truth and ultimate meaning, which are worth fighting and dying for, a reality vividly portrayed in the relationship between the ardent atheist, James Turnbull, and the devout Roman Catholic, Evan MacIan, in Chesterton's *The Ball and The Cross*.

Turnbull is the publisher of a paper in which he writes articles exposing what he believes to be the false claims and fundamental contradictions of Christian theology. On the front window of his shop he posts articles proposing to undermine the very foundation of life for the Christian citizens of London, and yet,

> He had said the worst thing that could be said; and it seemed accepted and ignored like the ordinary second best of the politicians. Every day his blasphemies looked more glaring, and every day the dust lay thicker upon them. It made him feel as if he were moving in a world of idiots. He seemed among a race of men who smiled when told of their own death, or looked vacantly at the Day of Judgement. Year after year went by, and year after year the death of God in a shop in Ludgate became a less and less important occurrence.[11]

Many years go by as the good Christian people of London daily pass by Turnbull's blasphemies with indifference, "and at last a man came by who treated Mr. Turnbull's secularist shop with a real respect and seriousness. He was a young man in a grey plaid, and he smashed the window."[12] He smashes the glass and challenges Turnbull to a duel because he understands the article to be an attempt to undermine the one truth on which the possibility of true human flourishing depends. Then, at the smashing of the window and the furious threat from MacIan, "A great light like dawn came into Mr. Turnbull's face. Behind his red hair and beard he turned deadly pale with pleasure. Here, after twenty lone years of useless toil, he had his reward."[13]

11. Chesterton, *The Ball and The Cross*, 14
12. Ibid
13. Chesterton, *The Ball and The Cross*, 15

Turnbull and MacIan are enemies at first sight but have one thing in common. They understand that the pursuit of truth—particularly truth about God—is more important than anything else, which is a view that seems as laughably absurd to the magistrate they're taken to as it does to many Western people a century after Chesterton wrote. In response to MacIan's calling Turnbull an "enemy of God," the magistrate responds: "Be quiet. It is most undesirable that things of that sort should be spoken about—a—in public, and in an ordinary Court of Justice. Religion is—a—too personal a matter to be mentioned in such a place."[14] After MacIan goes on to explain that which provoked his violent response—that Turnbull "blasphemed Our Lady"—the magistrate continues with his high-minded chastisement: "I tell you once and for all! I tell you, once and for all, my man, that I will not have you turning on any religious rant or cant here. Don't imagine that it will impress me. The most religious people are not those who talk about it. (Applause.)"[15]

Chesterton makes it clear through the contrast between the two enemies and the court officials that, when it comes to religion, those who refrain from talking about it do so because they don't care about it. The truth about God is thought to be too hard to discern and the effort it requires inevitably leads to dissonance in one's self and with others. Therefore, it's best to keep quiet and sacrifice truth for peace. This approach to the religious question is the moral and intellectual equivalent of a young man who, when faced with the monumental decision of whether to propose marriage to the beautiful woman he's been dating, finds the question too daunting and decides instead to stop thinking about it and just drink beer and play video games. Such is the mental atmosphere many early twenty-first century Westerners find themselves in. It is a mindset undergirded by scientism that provides a type of Valium comfort where the world is less stressful because it is less real.

Richard Dawkins famously said in his *Blind Watchmaker* that Darwin made it possible to be an intellectually fulfilled atheist.

14. ibid
15. ibid

That Which is Stronger Than Sorrow or Joy

If one takes Darwin's theory to be an affirmation of naturalist philosophy, then Darwin also makes it possible to live a morally indifferent, passionless life. God and truth are worth living and fighting for; randomly evolved instincts are not. Evan MacIan, on the other hand, personifies the voice deep in the soul of every human being which says that life is *about* something that is utterly real and right—that the fulfillment of yearnings for perfect beauty, love, truth and justice must be realized. Those who are deafened to this voice cannot know the purpose for living and fighting rooted in the reality of God, which he explains in his response to the magistrate:

> I have no mother; I have no wife. I have only that which the poor have equally with the rich; which the lonely have equally with the man of many friends. To me this whole strange world is homely, because in the heart of it there is a home; to me this cruel world is kindly, because higher than the heavens there is something more human than humanity. If a man must not fight for this, may he fight for anything?[16]

The most real things are always primarily immaterial things. When, as so often happens in romantic stories, a man says to the woman he's in love with, "What happened between us . . . I just want you to know . . . that was real"—he definitely does not mean, "I just want you to know that the simultaneous contact of all four of our lips really did initiate neural signals that triggered my reproductive hormones."

The quality of an experience which compels people to describe it as "real," "true," "weighty," "ecstatic," or "other worldly," is precisely the quality of transcendence—that is, the clear sense that the experience is connected with or illuminated by something that transcends our bodily instincts. It is the transcendent reality which moves people to live, fight, and die for something which they know to be real. This being the case, if a person believes that all human experiences can only ever be a matter of bodily instincts, then the sense of transcendence is always an illusion, and the real things

16. Chesterton, *The Ball and The Cross*, 21

in life are not so real after all. One would be no more "alive" after a first kiss than after a hundredth burp. Likewise, there would be no more reason to argue about the question of God or true ethical principles than about changing wind currents.

In light of the anesthetic effect of scientism, an exchange between Turnbull and MacIan later in the story makes perfect sense: After leaving the pseudo-sensible magistrate, Turnbull and MacIan agree that their duel must take place as it is warranted by the colossal importance of the Truth and the question of God. But they soon find themselves once again in trouble with the police. Each time an appropriate setting is found to follow through with the fight, they're forced to abandon the attempt to evade the approaching authorities. As they speed through London in a horse-drawn coach, MacIan says to his erstwhile enemy with whom he is beginning an ironic friendship,

> I have been looking at all the streets as we went past, I have been looking at all the shops as we went past, I have been looking at all the churches as we went past. At first, I felt a little dazed with the vastness of it all. I could not understand what it all meant. But now I know exactly what it all means. It means us. This whole civilization is only a dream. You and I are the realities.[17]

Turnbull and MacIan are the vivid realities against the backdrop of a tranquil gray civilization because they are two men alive in a dead world.[18]

ADAM WAYNE

Along with Innocent Smith who is the "manalive" in Chesterton's book of that title, the protagonist who lives most vividly and vibrantly against the backdrop of a dead, colorless world is Adam Wayne, the Napoleon of Notting Hill. Chesterton writes the book

17. Chesterton, *The Ball and The Cross*, 30
18. In light of what's been argued throughout this book, Turnbull, the atheist, exemplifies an implicit contradiction in passionately fighting for the Truth while claiming there is no Divine source of Truth to align with.

in the first decade of the twentieth century and sets the story in a futuristic London of the 1980's where,

> The people had absolutely lost faith in revolutions. All revolutions are doctrinal—such as the French one, or the one that introduced Christianity. For it stands to common sense that you cannot upset all existing things, customs, and compromises, unless you believe in something outside them, something positive and divine. Now, England, during this century, lost all belief in this. It believed in a thing called Evolution.[19]

The story begins with three government officials, two of whom are mechanically businesslike, and the other, Auberon Quin, is, much to the consternation of his two colleagues, one who "cares for nothing but a joke,"[20] a man "whose soul has been emptied of all pleasures but folly."[21] In stark contrast, the bloodless businessman, Wilfrid Lambert, embodies the late twentieth century zeitgeist Chesterton envisions: "He had a great amount of intellectual capacity, of that peculiar kind which raises a man from throne to throne and lets him die loaded with honors without having either amused or enlightened the mind of a single man."[22]

The English government of which Lambert is a functionary has also discontinued the traditional means of enthroning a monarch from a royal family line and instead adopted an alternative approach by which the king is chosen from the public at random. "All hereditary monarchies were a matter of luck," explains Lambert's like-minded friend, Mr. Barker, and "so are alphabetical monarchies."[23] At one point early in the story, the three of them find themselves on a hilltop in sight of several Londoners observing quite a scene when Auberon Quin intentionally takes a figure of speech literally and stands on his head, much to the embarrassment of his two stolid colleagues. As he proceeds with more absurd

19. Chesterton, *The Napoleon of Notting Hill*, 6
20. ibid
21. G.K. Chesterton, *The Napoleon of Notting Hill*, 23
22. ibid
23. ibid

antics, two government officials ascend the hill and announce that Quin had been chosen as the new monarch of Great Britain.

Later, as the British crown has extended the horizon of possibilities for Quin's follies, he devises what he conceives as the greatest of his jokes. In a speech given to the London Society for the Recovery of Antiques, the king decrees that all boroughs of London must return to the decorum of medieval Europe, building city walls with gates that close at sunset complete with a well-armed city guard. Each borough will be identified with its own standard and colors, and all government officials will be required to dress in full courtly regalia with swords and plumes, always in their respective borough colors, and must travel with full entourage of heralders and standard bearers. As the king ends his speech, various members of the audience respond with laughter, confusion, and indignation, but it is said that "one pale face with burning blue eyes remained fixed upon the lecturer, and after the lecture a red-haired boy ran out of the room."[24]

The farce of medieval heraldry imposed on modern businessmen goes on for years, giving the king a sense of ironic triumph in countering the soulless pragmatism of the officials as he "never really enjoyed the full richness of the medieval garments unless the people compelled to wear them were very angry and businesslike."[25] One official arrives in a fluster as he is late for a meeting for lack of space in a cab to fit his heralders. At one point, however, the king realizes that, though his joke impedes the businessmen's pursuit of profit and efficiency, it also removes an impediment to something immensely more important.

The provost of North Kensington comes to the king in a fury over an unexpected obstacle to a project for new road construction, complaining that the recently appointed provost of Notting Hill refuses to allow the road to proceed through his borough, even though, "the only part that is really in question is one dirty little street—Pump Street—a street with nothing in it but a public-house

---

24. G.K. Chesterton, *The Napoleon of Notting Hill*, 34
25. ibid

and a penny toy-shop, and that sort of thing."[26] The other provosts join in, all concurring with their indignant colleague. As the tension rises, it is announced that Adam Wayne has arrived. He was the boy so fixated on the king's speech years earlier and is now the provost of Notting Hill. In the midst of the scoffing businessmen, he flings his sword on the ground, kneels on one knee behind it, and gives homage to the king.

At first Auberon Quin relishes Wayne's full and convincing participation in the joke, and then is taken aback upon realizing that to him it is not a joke. We soon learn that Adam Wayne,

> was one of those to whom nature has given the desire without the power of artistic expression. He had been a mute poet from his cradle . . . [and then, at the king's decree] this one man found himself in the midst of a heraldic vision, in which he could act and speak and live lyrically. While the author and the victims alike treated the whole matter as a silly public charade, this one man, by taking it seriously, sprang suddenly into a throne of artistic omnipotence.[27]

The banners, standards, swords, and plumes enable Wayne to "live lyrically" because they are a means of expressing the inarticulate knowledge of the heart. He knows something the calculating businessmen with their quotidian hearts do not, and for that he is willing to fight. The king is confused because he sees that the business of the businessmen is so inconsequential—so incongruent with the soul—that it should not be taken with such seriousness, but he does not know what should.

He turns sober-minded for the first time in the story and questions Adam Wayne in an attempt to make sense of what appears to everyone else as nonsense. Wayne's response is one of the most soul-stirring passages in all of Chesterton's work, and it is to the mind sedated by scientism what filet mignon and Merlot are to a person at the end of a long fast:

26. ibid

27. Chesterton, *The Napoleon of Notting Hill*, 58 (Also, in British English, "dumb" is used for "mute.")

> "There is something in what you say," said [the king]. "You seem to have been thinking, young man."
>
> "Only feeling, sire," answered the Provost. "I was born, like other men, in a spot of the earth which I loved because I had played boys' games there, and fallen in love, and talked with my friends through nights that were nights of the gods. And I feel the riddle. These little gardens where we told our loves. These streets where we brought out our dead. Why should they be commonplace? Why should they be absurd? Why should it be grotesque to say that a pillar-box is poetic when for a year I could not see a red pillar-box against the yellow evening in a certain street without being wracked with something of which God keeps the secret, but which is stronger than sorrow or joy? Why should anyone be able to raise a laugh by saying 'the Cause of Notting Hill'?— Notting Hill where thousands of immortal spirits blaze with alternate hope and fear."

The secret God keeps is an open secret. It is a secret because we cannot access and observe it like the moon or water molecules. But it is the most open of secrets because by it "we live and move and have our being."[28] It is the "life that is truly life"[29] which manifests in wedding gowns and funeral flowers—in high ceilings and high honors—and it is the only life that makes people alive in the most meaningful sense of the word.

This life is a sun; love, beauty, and justice are its rays, and it is the source of an inarticulate knowledge that is the ballast of hope and sanity in an insane world. It is that which wracks the soul with something "stronger than sorrow or joy," and it cannot be captured and quantified by scientific calculations any more than the Leviathan can be caught with a fishhook.[30]

---

28. Acts 17:28. This is The Apostle Paul likely quoting the Cretan philosopher Epimenides of Knossos as Paul explains to the philosophers in Athens that the unknown God who is the ground of being has made himself known in the person of Christ.

29. 1 Timothy 6:19

30. Job 41:1

That Which is Stronger Than Sorrow or Joy

Adam Wayne lives in light of this life. Reveling in impractical plumage and heraldry, he is the mute poet who knows much more than he can tell. In his impractical passion to defend the mundane things which are a conduit of the sacred, he is a man alive, rising like a lucid flame out of the ash heap of the hopeless world that, according to Bertrand Russel, must be our habitation if we are to live only in view of that which "science presents for our belief."[31]

---

31. Russell, "A Free Man's Worship," first published as "The Free Man's Worship," Dec. 1903

Bibliography

Augustine, *Confessions*. Translated by Sarah Ruden. Reprint, Modern Library. New York: Random House, 2017.
Berger, Peter L. *A Rumor of Angels; Modern Society and the Rediscovery of the Supernatural*. Garden City, NY: Doubleday, 1969.
Bradbury, Ray. *Fahrenheit 451*. New York: Simon and Schuster, 2013.
Chesterton, G.K. *The Autobiography of G.K. Chesterton*. San Francisco: Ignatius, 2006.
———. *The Ball and The Cross*. New York: John Lane Company, 1909.
———. *Charles Dickens*. London: Methuen, 1949.
———. *The Club of Queer Trades*. New York: Harper, 1905.
———. *The Defendant*. Mineola: Dover, 2012.
———. *The Everlasting Man*. San Francisco: Ignatius, 1993.
———. *The Flying Inn*. New York: John Lane Company, 1914.
———. *Heretics*. New York: John Lane, 1905.
———. "Leviathan and the Hook." *The Speaker*, September 9, 1905.
———. *Manalive*. San Francisco: Ignatius, 2011.
———. *The Napoleon of Notting Hill*. London: John Lane Company, 1904.
———. *Orthodoxy*. San Francisco: Ignatius, 1995.
———. "The Philosophy of First Thoughts," *The Speaker*, September 14, 1901.
———. *The Poet and The Lunatics: Episodes in the Life of Gabriel Gale*. Mineola: Dover, 2010.
———. *Robert Louis Stevenson*. New York: Dodd, Mead and Company, 1928.
———. *Saint Francis of Assisi*. London: Hodder and Stoughton, 1923.
———. "Straight Thinking," London Daily News, February 2, 1905.
———. *The Superstition of Divorce*. New York: John Lane Company, 1920.
———. *Tremendous Trifles*. Mineola: Dover, 2007.
Coates, John. *Chesterton and the Edwardian Cultural Crisis*. Leiden: Brill, 1986.
Dalrymple, Theodore, *Our Culture, What's Left of It*. London: Monday, 2010.
Dawkins, Richard. *Climbing Mount Improbable*. New York: Norton and Company, 1996.
Descartes, René. *Discourse on Method and Meditations on First Philosophy*. Indianapolis: Hackett, 1988.

Bibliography

Dostoyevsky, Fyodor. *The Brothers Karamazov*. London: Penguin, 2003.

Howard, Thomas. *Chance or the Dance? 2nd Edition: A Critique of Modern Secularism*. San Francisco: Ignatius, 2001.

Jaki, Stanley L. *Chesterton, a Seer of Science*. Pinckney: Real View, 2001.

Kerr, Ian. *G.K. Chesterton: A Biography*. Oxford: Oxford UP, 2011.

Lauer, Quentin. *G. K. Chesterton: Philosopher without Portfolio*. New York: Fordham UP, 1991.

Lewis, C. S. "The Empty Universe," in *Present Concerns*: San Francisco, 1996.

———. *Miracles: A Preliminary Study*. Touchstone, 1996.

———. *Perelandra*. New York: Scribner, 1996.

———. *The Pilgrim's Regress*. Grand Rapids: Eerdmans, 1992.

Nietzsche, Friedrich. *The Gay Science*. Translated by Walter Kaufmann. New York: Random House, 1974.

Pinker, Steven: *Enlightenment Now, The Case for Reason, Science, Humanism, and Progress*. Penguin Random House: London, 2018.

Plantinga, Alvin. *Warranted Christian Belief*. New York: Oxford University Press, 2000.

———. *Where the Conflict Really Lies: Science, Religion, and Naturalism*. New York: Oxford UP, 2011.

Polanyi, Michael. *Personal Knowledge; towards a Post-critical Philosophy*. University of Chicago Press, 1958.

———. *The Tacit Dimension*. University of Chicago Press: 2009.

Reyburn, Duncan. *Seeing Things as They Are G.K. Chesterton and the Drama of Meaning*. Eugene, OR: Cascade, 2016.

Russell, Bertrand, Albert C. Lewis, and Alasdair Urquhart. *The Collected Papers of Bertrand Russell*. London: Routledge, 1994.

Singer, Peter. *Practical Ethics*, 2nd Ed. Cambridge University Press, 1993.

Spitzer, Robert. *The Soul's Upward Yearning: Clues to Our Transcendent Nature from Experience and Reason*. San Francisco: Ignatius, 2015.

Tolstoy, Leo, *The Death of Ivan Ilyich*. New York: Bantam, 1981.

Contact the author with questions or comments about the book at truthbeforelogic@gmail.com

www.ingramcontent.com/pod-product-compliance
Lightning Source LLC
Chambersburg PA
CBHW071214160426
43196CB00012B/2297